WISCONSIN

The Story of the Badger State

Norman K. Risjord

Wisconsin Trails
Madison, Wisconsin

Library of Congress Catalog Card Number: 95-61444
ISBN 0-915024-49-7

Design by Kathie Campbell. Edited by Elizabeth McBride.
Printed in the United States of America by BookCrafters.

The publisher gratefully acknowledges the State Historical Society
of Wisconsin for the use of its photographs. Photo on page 126 courtesy
of the Milwaukee Public Museum. Photo on page 195 courtesy of the
Milwaukee Journal. Photo on page 214 by Jeff Miller, courtesy of
University of Wisconsin-Madison News and Public Affairs.
Maps by the University of Wisconsin-Madison Cartographic Laboratory.
Cover photo: Cornish cottage at Pendarvis, Mineral Point, by Terry Donnelly.

Wisconsin Trails
P.O. Box 5650
6225 University Ave.
Madison, WI 53705

For my son, Eric.
No one loves more deeply
Wisconsin's lakes and woodlands.

Workers raise "Forward" onto the dome of the Capitol, July 1914.

CONTENTS

PREFACE

One of the joys of retirement is that one feels free to turn from pioneering scholarship to popular history. The story of the Badger State, recounted here, was a labor of love. It was written with people who "hate history" in mind, and I hope that I have brought alive for them the story of Wisconsin's development from glacial tundra to complex, modern society.

My wife Connie played the role of "common man," giving the manuscript a careful reading from a nonscholar's point of view, and her suggestions greatly improved the narrative. Margaret Bogue, my colleague in retirement from the the University of Wisconsin-Madison Department of History, gave the manuscript a scholarly critique, updating my interpretations and correcting my errors. To both of them I am deeply indebted.

Norman K. Risjord
Richland County,
Spring 1995

Chapter 1

THE CREEPING WALL OF ICE

T he story of modern Wisconsin begins with ice, a moving mountain of ice that scoured the countryside and rearranged the hills and valleys. It is called the Wisconsin glacier because of the profound impact it had on the Badger State, and it was the last of four glaciers that have overrun North America in the last million years. It occurred relatively recently, as geologic time goes. About 30,000 years ago the earth began to cool off, after experiencing a relatively warm climate since the previous (Illinois) glacier. The reasons for the gradual cooling are not fully understood. One theory holds that an expansion of the permanent ice sheets in the Arctic and Antarctic reflected back into space a significant amount of the sun's energy, thus preventing the earth from receiving its normal summertime warming effect. Whatever the cause, by 27,000 years ago Wisconsin was under permafrost. Animal life had moved south, the trees had disappeared, and the landscape was a tundra of lichens and moss.

▼

The Glacier's Advance

The Wisconsin glacier originated in the Canadian highlands east of Hudson Bay. Snow, brought in by moist air from the south and east, accumulated in ever-greater depths. Partial melting in the summertime changed the snowflakes from filigreed crystals into tiny balls of ice. The weight of additional layers pressed the balls into a hard mass. The layering of snow and ice continued year after year, century after century. When the ice mass reached about 200 feet in height, it began to move. The great weight of the glacier, together with heat from the center of the earth, melted the ice at the bottom and produced a thin film of water under the ice. Sliding on this film, the bottom ice oozed outward, creaking and groaning, while new snow and ice accumulated at the surface of the glacier. The movement was slow at first, but as the glacier worked southward onto the level lands around the Great Lakes it increased to 200 or 300 feet a year.

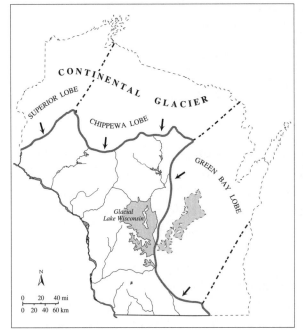

The Driftless Area at the Wisconsin stage of glaciation.

The ice mass, with its brethren in western Canada and northern Europe, further cooled the earth's climate, as its glassy surface acted like a mirror that shot the sun's rays back into space. The Ice Age was self-perpetuating. The glacier eventually reached a depth of two miles in central Canada, and its weight was such that it compressed the earth's crust, creating a huge dent in the earth itself.

The moving ice picked up sand, gravel, rocks and even huge boulders, absorbing them into the glacier. The sliding mixture scoured the earth and picked up even more debris. With a rasping sound, it scraped off the thin soil that covered Canada's granitelike bedrock, and sandpapered even that hard rock until the surface was round and smooth. When the leading edge of the ice reached present-day Lake Superior, it found a rift or crack in the earth's crust. It flowed downward into the rift and scooped out the basin down to the bedrock, some 730 feet below sea level. The lake has since filled in with sand and silt, but its contours were formed by the glacier. To the east, about 23,000 years ago, the moving ice encountered an ancient river bed, and a lobe of the glacier followed that southward to carve out Lake Michigan.

The creeping ice could be deflected by high, hard outcroppings. One such was the Niagara escarpment that forms present-day Door County at Green Bay. This wedge of hard rock, formed in the hot core of the earth and thrust to the surface by the movement of the earth's crust, threads east from Green Bay to Niagara Falls and south to Lake Winnebago. The escarpment split the Lake Michigan Lobe and caused a new lobe to begin moving southwest across Wisconsin. This mass of ice—the Green Bay Lobe—had the most dramatic effect of all on the landscape of the state. It gouged out Green Bay, Lake Winnebago and the Horicon Marsh. It was guided by the Niagara escarpment as far as the bottom of Lake Winnebago, but south of that it was free to expand to east and west. Pushing to the east, the Green Bay Lobe ran into the expanding Lake Michigan lobe. Like two huge bulldozers, the ice sheets formed a mountain chain of rocky debris, now known as the Kettle Moraine.

To the west, the Green Bay Lobe stopped just short of present-day Wausau and Stevens Point, its limit marked by a line of boulders and gravel (called a "moraine"), some of which had been pushed all the way from Canada. (Some Wisconsin moraines contain diamonds that appear to have originated in the Hudson Bay region, although the source has never been found.) From Stevens Point the moraine runs south to Baraboo, Prairie du Sac, and to a point just west of Madison near Cross Plains and Verona. It thus enveloped the eastern half of the Baraboo Hills, though the hardrock hills were themselves not much affected by the ice. As fate would have it, the lobe stopped at the one watergap in the hills, through which an ancient river had once flowed, the site of present-day Devil's Lake. The moraine plugged the gap and turned the Baraboo Hills into a natural dam when the ice began to melt. South of Madison the Green Bay Lobe stopped just short of Janesville, and to the east it merged with the Lake Michigan Lobe, which was pushing into northern Illinois.

While the Green Bay Lobe sculpted eastern Wisconsin, the Lake Superior Lobe spread across the northern part of the state and into Minnesota. Slowed by the northern highlands (today the Laurentian Divide that splits the waters flowing northeast to the Atlantic from those flowing south into the Gulf of Mexico), the Lake Superior Lobe did not advance much in a southerly direction before the Ice Age came to an end. Its terminal moraine ran roughly from Merrill to Chippewa Falls and Hudson. The portion of Wisconsin south and west of these two glacial lobes is known as the Driftless Area because the landscape shows none of the effects of glaciation (though it may have been once covered by a previous glacier). Why the Driftless Area was spared the effects of ice when a lobe to the west of it was covering southern Minnesota and Iowa has been the subject of much speculation. The best answer seems to be that the ice, like water, followed natural depressions in the landscape, such as lakes Superior and Michigan. By the time the glacier turned its attention to the higher lands of southwestern Wisconsin, the climate was warming once again and the ice began to melt.

At its apex, about 18,000 years ago, the glacier covered Wisconsin, except for the Driftless Area, with an icecap about 400 feet thick. From the air it would have appeared as a glistening white, featureless plain, with occasional islands of tundra—Rib Mountain, the Baraboo Hills—poking up through the ice. At the edge of each lobe was a dirty gray mixture of rocks and ice, and beyond that a flood plain of silt and sand broken by trickling rivulets of water. A mass of frigid air hovered above the ice, sending wintry fronts rippling to the south and east. The tundra extended south of the glacier for many miles; the forest of spruce and birch now associated with northern Wisconsin retreated beyond the Ohio River.

The climate began to warm about that time, though it was another thousand years before the glacier began to retreat. The intervening period of "dead ice" was far from dead. It groaned under stress and broke apart with sharp *thwacks* that sounded like a clap of thunder. When the ice thinned to about 200 feet, cracks and fissures appeared that reached to the bottom of the glacier. During the summer, when most of the melting occurred, water gurgled into these openings, carrying debris along. As the water reached the bottom of the ice, it spread out and created a cone-shaped hole. When the ice finally retreated, the debris in these holes became permanent features of the landscape: conical hills called "kames," and oval or elongated hills called "drumlins." Sometimes the water flowed under the ice from one pond to the next, carrying sand and gravel in a sinuous line and forming an "esker." These glacial features are particularly prominent in the Kettle Moraine area. Sometimes the fissures caused huge chunks of ice to break off altogether and become buried amidst the rock and gravel of the moraine. When the blocks melted they left rounded ponds of water that reminded the first observers of kitchen kettles or pots; hence the name "Kettle Moraine."

▼

The Great Melt

The retreat began in earnest about 15,000 years ago. In places where it can be measured, the ice front drew back at a rate of several hundred feet a year. But the retreat was by no means uniform. The ice might withdraw for a century or two and then, during a short-term change of climate, come creeping back again. An example of what could happen can be seen today at the famous Two Creeks Forest Bed on the shore of Lake Michigan north of Manitowoc. There wave action has exposed layers of glacial drift. Sandwiched between thick layers of red clay till is a brown layer of forest soil with still-visible pine cones and needles. In this layer are well-preserved spruce logs, some of which had been growing for a hundred years or more. Clearly, the glacier had returned and ambushed a premature forest. Carbon dating allows us to time the Two Creeks forest with some precision; it was buried 11,850 years ago.

The end moraines marked the farthest reach of the Wisconsin

lobes, but the irregular retreat of the ice left a series of "recessional" moraines that further pocked the landscape. One such is on the south shore of Lake Mendota, where the University of Wisconsin resides. A drumlin, formed by a hole in the melting glacier, is the site of the State Capitol.

Esker in the Kettle Moraine State Forest near Parnell.

Forty miles north of the capital the Baraboo Hills, whose one gap had been plugged by the moraine, formed a gigantic dam for the glacial melt. Over a period of two or three thousand years a lake formed behind the dam ("Glacial Lake Wisconsin") that stretched north almost to Stevens Point and west to Tomah and Eau Claire. The lake level varied over the centuries as it found various outlets to the northwest, the principal one being by way of the Black River to the Mississippi. Although the northwestern part of the lake was quite shallow, it deepened to about 75 feet in the Baraboo area. Mill Bluff State Park, near Camp Douglas, contains several spectacular examples of sandstone pillars, one-time islands in the lake that had been shaped into their present form by the action of the waves. South of the Baraboo Hills the terminal moraine stopped other waters at the site of present-day Prairie du Sac, creating a lake that geologists have named Lake Merrimac and is commonly referred to as Lake Wisconsin. Lake Merrimac was about 30 meters below the level of Glacial Lake Wisconsin.

We have only an approximate date for the draining of Glacial Lake Wisconsin and the emergence of the "sand counties" from the former lake bed—some 14,000 years ago. We know with much greater precision how long it took—about three days, at least for the initial cataclysm. As the waters of the glacial lake rose steadily it was inevitable that they would eventually attack the pile of rock and gravel that formed the plug. Once the water started to flow across the moraine it cut rapidly into the loose debris, and one arm of Lake Wisconsin spilled into Lake Merrimac in a matter of days. The catastrophic flood carried meter-sized boulders downstream for almost 10 miles, and a delta of gravel formed at the edge of Lake Merrimac. (The site of the breakthrough is roughly the interchange between Highway 78 and Interstate 90/94 today.) The main lake drained much more slowly, but the currents gradually cut away at the soft sandstone to the north and west of the Baraboo Hills. The result was a narrow gorge and a new channel for the Wisconsin River, which in preglacial times had flowed farther to the west. Over the centuries the river cut ever deeper into the sandstone, creating the formation now known as the Wisconsin Dells.

When the Superior and Michigan lobes melted, about 10,000 to 12,000 years ago, they left a gigantic lake, perhaps the largest freshwater lake ever formed. It included lakes Huron, Michigan and Superior, and its waters extended north and west into Manitoba. Lake Winnipeg and the Lake of the Woods are remnants of glacial Lake Algonquin, as geologists have named it. As with Lake Wisconsin, the outlets of this freshwater sea varied with time and water level. One arm, Lake Duluth, spilled into the St. Croix River and thence into the Mississippi. Lake Michigan, for a time, drained south into the Mississippi. The removal of the ice lifted a great weight from the earth's crust, which slowly began a rebound. The rising land closed the outlets to the west and south and forced the waters to turn east. For a time they flowed by way of the Ottawa River to the St. Lawrence. When rising land and receding lake level closed that waterway, the waters from the upper lakes developed a more circuitous route to the St. Lawrence through lakes Erie and Ontario.

By 8,000 years ago the glacier had retreated to Hudson Bay. Rising ocean waters flowed into the bay and completed the breakup of the ice. In that basin too the earth's crust began to rebound. Indeed, the land is still rising, and eventually, unless the ocean levels rise due to global warming, Hudson Bay will disappear.

The shriveling ice left behind a barren wasteland, but not for long. The Driftless Area was a seedbed for pioneer vegetation, ferns and lichens, which moved quickly onto the fertile silt in the glacial outwash. Spruce, pine and birch soon followed. The experience of the ambushed spruce forest at the Two Creeks Bed indicates how early the forest cover returned to the Wisconsin landscape. The lush vegetation attracted grazing animals, and hunters with stone-tipped spears followed soon after.

▼

North America's First Inhabitants

The peopling of North America had begun even while ice ruled the land. So much of the earth's water supply was tied up in ice during the 10,000 years of the Wisconsin glacier that the level of the oceans fell by as much as 300 feet below where they are now. In the shallow straits that separated Alaska from Siberia, the dropping seas opened up a land bridge for both animals and humans. Indeed, it was more than a "bridge," for the dry land connection was about 1,500 miles wide and embraced most of the western coast of Alaska. Such a corridor afforded ample room for the slow exchange of plants and animals, and when the first human hunters followed the game across the bridge, they probably never realized they were crossing from one continent to another.

At the time the Ice Age began, North America already supported an astonishing menagerie of wildlife. The principal newcomer coming across the land bridge was the bison, which had evolved in Asia. Already present were the mastodon, a variety of elephants, several kinds of saber-toothed cat, horse, camel, bear, antelope and jaguar. Smaller animals that had evolved into their modern form included the beaver, fox, skunk, otter, raccoon, badger, rabbit and mouse. The large animals, which lost body heat more slowly than the small ones, survived the Ice Age well, but, ironically, many of them became extinct at the end of the glacial period.

It was probably this diversity of animal life that attracted the first human hunters. Siberia, though desperately cold, was only partially covered with ice because of the shortage of snowfall. Thus it sustained a human population, pushed there no doubt by pressure from migrating tribes to the south and west. The humans would have learned how to build shelters and garb themselves in furs for warmth; they were thus already well adapted to the conditions they would meet in Alaska and Canada.

The best evidence we have that the native inhabitants of North America originated in Asia is blood type. Nearly all pure-blooded American Indians have type-O blood, which is also the dominant blood type of the people of northeastern Asia. The uniformity of blood type also suggests a rather small gene pool. It is likely that the migrants across the Alaskan land bridge numbered only in the tens of thousands. Reproduction brought this number up into the millions by the time of the European discovery.

A nearly perfect glacial kame near Dundee.

The first nomads appeared about 20,000 years ago, at a time when the ice was still creeping into Wisconsin. In central Alaska they encountered familiar conditions, for the heart of Alaska is dry, like Siberia, and suffered little or no glaciation. They thrived, and perhaps multiplied, in the valley of the Yukon River, which led them eastward into Canada. But, for the moment, they could go no farther because another ice sheet had developed in the mountains of the Pacific Northwest. Fed by the torrential snows of the Cascade Range, this glacier spread north to the Aleutian Islands and east across the plains until it connected with a lobe of the Laurentian (Wisconsin) glacier. However, when ice sheets began to recede, an ice-free corridor developed in western Canada, linking the unglaciated part of Alaska with the heartland of the continent. Human migrants moved down this pathway, finding an evermore congenial environment. A large part of present-day Nevada and Utah was then covered by a huge glacial lake, of which the Great Salt Lake is a remnant, and the lake was surrounded by grasslands. Hunting and fishing must have been excellent. Although these people were equipped only with stone-tipped spears (later migrants would bring the bow and arrow), they must have learned how to hunt animals by setting fires or herding them into box canyons.

The southern movement of population was fairly brisk by geologic standards. The Great Plains were then covered with a pine forest, and kill sites indicate the presence of big-game hunters there between 11,000 and 13,000 years ago. Spear points and the charred bones of animals indicate a human presence in Mexico by 11,000 years ago.

Accompanying the human migration, though not necessarily caused by it, was the disappearance of most of the large animals that had given the New World such rich diversity. Interestingly, marine life was not affected during the great die-off, nor were small mammals. But by the end of the Ice Age 8,000 years ago, the only large mammals on the continent were the moose, bear, deer and bison. Gone forever were the elephant, mastodon, giant beaver, saber-toothed cat, camel and horse. The llama, a relative of the camel, preserved itself only by retreating to the Andes Mountains of South

America. Some ecologists have blamed human predation, but it seems unlikely that hunters armed with spears could have brought about such a massive extinction. The best explanation at present is that the large animals were weakened by the continual changes in habitat due to the advance and recession of the glacier. Human predation, which was probably most successful with females and the young, may have been the coup de grace.

▼

Wisconsin's Early Hunters and Nomads

Mastodons and other large grazing animals moved into Wisconsin shortly after the ice receded, feeding on the lush grasses that grew on the glacial till. Human hunters followed them eastward from the Great Plains. The first arrivals appeared about 10,000 years ago. We know these people only by their weapons, for spear points are the only evidence we have of their passing. These spear points were large and of chipped stone. The most distinctive feature was a carved channel, or "flute," in the center of the piece, carved out to hold a shaft or handle. Clovis-fluted points (named for a site in New Mexico where they were first discovered) have been found throughout the Upper Great Lakes region. These people almost certainly made their living by hunting, for the climate was still too cold to grow crops. They were thus nomadic of necessity, and their clothing and shelter were probably made of skins. Their culture disappeared about 7,000 years ago when the climate became warmer and the mastodons disappeared. Some of the Clovis people may have moved farther north in search of game; those who remained would have had to adjust to new arrivals with a different hunting technology.

The next group also came from the Plains, where their spear points have been found alongside bison remains. These hunters were equipped with long, thin and sharp spear points, chipped from hard stone. The shaft was attached to a groove at the butt end. These were lake people, who lived on shorelines or small islands, which suggests that they lived by fishing as well as hunting. The mastodons had vanished by then, but deer, elk and caribou were still abundant. They placed weapons, tools and ornaments in graves with their dead, which indicates that they believed in a supernatural life after death.

For about 5,000 years before the birth of Christ, when civilizations were emerging in Egypt, Mesopotamia and China, Wisconsin was inhabited by woodland Indians who had developed, in addition to spear points, a variety of woodworking tools, such as the axe, the adz and the gouge. Instead of being chipped into shape, these tools were ground smooth and given a sharp cutting edge. Their spears had small, sharp points and thin shafts for easy throwing. Some had an added handle midway down the shaft, which gave the thrower a whiplike action that added speed and distance. Like the earlier hunters, these people were nomadic: small bands united by ties of kinship roving over a large territory.

▼

Copper Culture

During this same time period, there appeared along the shorelines of the Upper Great Lakes a unique people. We do not know whether they were newcomers or offspring of their nomadic neighbors. What made them distinctive was their use of copper; they were the first fabricators of metal in the Americas and perhaps in the whole world. At first, no doubt, they simply picked up globs of copper lying on the forest floor along the shores of Lake Superior, where it could be found in some abundance. Exposure to heat (in a fire circle perhaps?) demonstrated its metallic properties, and only a modicum of ingenuity was required to fashion the molten metal into a tool. When they exhausted the surface wealth, they dug mines and fired the ore to extract the pure metal. There are thousands of mining pits on the Keweenaw Peninsula of Michigan, some of them at least 20 deep. Mining sites and charcoal pits can also be found along the shores of Green Bay and Lake Michigan, and in the Fox River Valley. They fashioned the copper into spear points, knives and woodworking tools. Since there is no evidence of agricultural implements made of copper, the Copper Indians were probably hunters like their predecessors.

About 3000 B.C. the climate of North America became much warmer, warmer than at any time up to the present. The spruce forest retreated into Canada, and a hardwood forest of oak, hickory and chestnut conquered Wisconsin. Some of the Copper Indians seem to have followed the spruce forest and its inhabitants, cari-

Bear effigy mound near Lake Koshkonong.

bou and moose, to the north. Their most recent pits and firepoints were found on the shores of glacial Lake Agassiz in western Ontario. In the year 1771, an explorer in the northwestern part of Canada found Indians who had copper tools and weapons, so perhaps a remnant of their culture survived into historic times. Any Copper Indians who remained in Wisconsin by 500 B.C. probably adapted to the arrival of a new people with even more sophisticated technologies.

▼

The Mound Builders

Burial mounds and pottery were the identifying characteristics of the north-central Woodland culture in the first millennium after the birth of Christ. We do not know whether these techniques spread to Wisconsin by trade and imitation or whether they were brought by migrating peoples. Perhaps it was both. The mound-building culture was river-borne and southern in origin. Perhaps its techniques originated among the Indian civilizations of Mexico. The culture flowed north along the Mississippi and its tributaries, the Ohio, the Illinois and the Wisconsin.

The most interesting mounds in Wisconsin are effigy mounds, usually depicting mammals, birds or reptiles—often in groups and of gigantic size. Some eagles have a wingspread of 1,000 feet; other mounds depict panthers with tails 300 feet long. The effigies were probably totems. A family or clan felt it had a blood relationship with a certain species, and the animal in turn watched over and protected them. Explorers who encountered Wisconsin tribes in historic times found them subdivided into clans with names like Bear, Moose, Fox, Wolf, Panther or Lynx. Occasionally the figures were cut into the earth, and near them were hundreds of simple burial mounds.

Pottery was the other addition to the Great Lakes Woodland culture in the centuries after the birth of Christ. The pots were thick, wide-mouth jars decorated with impressions made on the clay by fabric, carved stones or shells. This sort of pottery was common among primitive peoples from Asia to northern Europe. The art may have come across the land bridge and filtered eastward.

▼

The Hopewell People

One immigrant group that arrived in Wisconsin early in this period (perhaps about the time of Christ), the Hopewell people, were accomplished mound builders and pottery makers. They were also farmers, traders and artists of exceptional ability. The Hopewell were a riverine people who settled along every major river in the mid-continent. (Their name is taken from a mound near Chillicothe, Ohio.) One branch of the culture, distinguished from other groups by its distinctive pottery, was centered on the Illinois River. With outlying settlements on the Rock and Wisconsin rivers, it cast a cultural shadow across southern Wisconsin. Because the Hopewell people depended primarily on agriculture, they remained in relatively warm climes. They grew corn, squash, beans and probably tobacco, all crops that required a lengthy growing season. We know that they either grew or traded for tobacco because their art work included pipes with nicely carved figurines.

Hopewell ceremonial pottery was the finest of any made in the western Great Lakes region. It was crafted of fired clay tempered with particles of limestone, which gave it a shiny gray appearance. Since this pottery has only been found in burial mounds, it was probably made for that purpose. The Hopewells had also mastered the art of weaving. Lacking looms, they worked by finger twining, using the soft inner bark of certain trees. Women fashioned the material into wrap-around skirts for themselves and breach cloths for their men.

▼

Mississippian Culture

By A.D. 700 the glory of the Hopewell culture had dimmed, but it was soon replaced by another river-oriented, mound-building culture from the south. Because its principal population centers were on the lower Mississippi River, scholars have named this the Mississippian culture. Like the earlier Hopewell people, the Mississippians were accustomed to a warm climate and practiced extensive agriculture. But as they moved into the northern woodlands, they adopted the economy of their neighbors, who lived by hunting, fishing, and gathering fruits in the woods. Chipped stone arrowheads found in campsites of this period indicate that the bow and arrow (probably invented in Asia) had at last reached Wisconsin.

The largest city of the Mississippian culture was Cahokia, located near the present town of East Saint Louis, Illinois. First settled around A.D. 800, the site eventually encompassed six square miles with more than 100 manmade mounds. The largest of these, built for religious ceremonies, covers 16 acres and rises in four terraces to a height of 100 feet. Cahokia was a major commercial as well as religious center, and it spawned a number of colonies, through the export of skilled workers and through imitation by neighboring Woodland peoples. The most important of these was Aztalan on the Rock River in southern Wisconsin, founded about A.D. 1100. Still quite visible today, Aztalan was protected by a fortified stockade with walkways that enclosed interior plazas and platform mounds. Scattered both inside and outside the stockade are the remains of dwellings, shallow excavations that at one time probably had superstructures of wood and bark. Firepits inside the dwellings are lined with clay. Refuse pits contain corn, squash and charred bones, some of them human. Among the artifacts that have been found at the site are ear pendants made from Gulf Coast shells and long-nosed god masks, which suggest extensive trade and cultural exchange. Aztalan was abandoned by the time Columbus discovered America; the mound-building culture had also died out by then.

▼

Winnebago Ancestors

The most important newcomers in this period, arriving about A.D. 1000, were people who came from the west and spoke a Sioux-related language. (Most other Wisconsin tribes present when the first Europeans arrived spoke Algonquian languages, similar to those of the tribes of Michigan and the St. Lawrence Valley.) The immigrants settled on the shores of Lake Winnebago and in the Fox River Valley. Ancestors of the Winnebago tribe, they made their living by hunting, farming, and fishing. They hunted with bow and arrow, as well as traps and snares. They had a wide variety of tools made from stone, wood and the bones of animals. They buried their dead in oblong grave pits in cemeteries. The dead went off to an afterlife well provided with tools, weapons, utensils and ornaments.

By the time the first European explorers arrived in the early 1600s, the Wisconsin tribes were part of a generalized Woodland culture that extended from the Upper Great Lakes to the Atlantic Coast. Algonquian was the dominant language group among the tribes, which suggests a fairly common crossing of the Alaskan land bridge. But it was a culture not at all prepared for the arrival of the white man, with his startling new technology, material temptations and communicable diseases.

▼

Travelers' Guide

Glacial Geology

Devil's Lake State Park, off Highway 12 south of Baraboo; (608) 356-8301. Five-hundred-foot bluffs formed 1.5 billion years ago surround a clear lake created by glacial action.

Ice Age National Scenic Trail, P.O. Box 423, Pewaukee, WI 53072; (800) 227-0046. Hiking path through Wisconsin follows the terminal moraine of the last glacier.

Interstate State Park, Highway 35 south of St. Croix; (715) 483-3747. View a deep gorge and whirlpool-formed potholes cut by glacial meltwaters. Ice Age Interpretive Center features exhibits and films.

Kettle Moraine State Forest, Northern Unit, Highway 67 between Plymouth and Campbellsport; (414) 626-2116. Southern Unit, Highway 59 between Palmyra and Eagle; (414) 594-6200. Both units contain outstanding glacial features, including kames, eskers and kettles. Learn about the region's glacial history at the Henry S. Reuss Ice Age Visitor Center, south of Dundee on Highway 57, and the Southern Unit's Visitor Center, three miles west of Eagle on Highway 59.

Mill Bluff State Park, Highway 12/16 between Camp Douglas and Tomah; (608) 427-6692. Imposing sandstone buttes were once islands in prehistoric Glacial Lake Wisconsin.

University of Wisconsin Geology Museum, Weeks Hall, 1215 W. Dayton St.; (608) 262-1412. This small museum houses rock exhibits, a re-creation of a limestone cave, and skeletons of dinosaurs and mastodons, some of which were unearthed in Wisconsin.

Ancient Indian Cultures

Aztalan State Park, Highway Q two miles east of Lake Mills; (414) 648-8774. Site of an ancient Indian village, with pyramid and burial mounds.

Henschel's Indian Museum, N 8661 Holstein Rd., Elkhart Lake;

(414) 876-3193. Private museum displays stone tools, points and pottery found on the Henschel family farm.

High Cliff State Park, Highway 55/114 east of Menasha; (414) 989-1106. Self-guided Indian Mounds Interpretive Trail leads to panther and buffalo effigy mounds.

Lizard Mound County Park, County A, West Bend: (414) 335-4445. Contains effigy mounds built between A.D. 400 and 1200.

Logan Museum of Anthropology, Beloit College, 700 College St., Beloit; (608) 363-2677. One of the region's strongest collections of Indian artifacts.

Milwaukee Public Museum, 800 W. Wells St., Milwaukee; (414) 278-2702. Permanent exhibit on Wisconsin Woodland Indians.

Natural Bridge State Park, Highway C south of Baraboo; (608) 356-8301. Sandstone arch shelters site inhabited 12,000 years ago.

Neville Public Museum, 210 Museum Place, Green Bay; (414) 448-4460. Permanent walk-through exhibit on Wisconsin's Ice Age and Paleo-Indian culture.

Roche a Cri State Park, Highway 13 two miles north of Adams/Friendship; (608) 339-6881. Features Indian petroglyphs and a sandstone outcropping that was once an island in Glacial Lake Wisconsin.

State Historical Museum, 30 N. Carroll St., Madison; (608) 264-6555. Permanent exhibit on Wisconsin Indian life.

Wyalusing State Park, Highway C south of Prairie du Chien; (608) 996-2261. Twenty-eight effigy mounds sit atop a ridge overlooking the Mississippi River.

Native American Mounds in Madison and Dane County. A free booklet detailing 20 mound sites accessible to the public is available at the Madison Public Library, 201 W. Mifflin St., and Madison's Department of Planning and Development, 215 Martin Luther King Jr. Blvd., Madison, WI 53703.

Chapter 2

FRENCH, FURS, INDIANS AND WAR

Both France and England coveted North America, but neither seemed to be in much of a hurry to occupy it. French and English explorers poked along the coast for 75 years before either country made a serious effort to establish a settlement. And then the "race" ended virtually in a tie. England established its first permanent settlement at Jamestown, Virginia, in 1607, and a year later the French founded Quebec on the St. Lawrence River.

The land-use strategies of the two settlements were markedly different, however. English colonists came as individuals, without government support or even encouragement. They arrived looking for opportunity; they came to cultivate and possess. The French settlement, on the other hand, was a royal enterprise; the first arrivals worked for the king and served his ends. And the targets of the French government in the 17th century were but two—the pelts of the woodland animals and the souls of the native inhabitants.

Because of these different strategies, the French and English empires developed in much different fashion. More than a century passed before the first Virginia exploring party reached the crest of the Blue Ridge, a mere 150 miles from the seacoast. By that time French explorers had long since penetrated the upper Great Lakes, and French trading posts at Green Bay and the Apostle Islands had mobilized the Indians into a single-minded hunt for furs.

▼

Arrival of the French

The Indians of the northeastern woodlands were divided into two great language groups, the Algonquian and the Iroquois. The Indians of the St. Lawrence Valley and the forests north of the Great Lakes spoke variations of the language of the Algonquins (the tribe that inhabited the upper St. Lawrence Valley and northern New England). The Algonquian tribes were nomadic people who primarily depended on hunting and fishing and lived in portable wigwams covered with bark or skins. The Iroquois, who evolved from a different prehistoric people, inhabited the region south and east of Lake Ontario in present-day New York. They were a sedentary, agricultural people who lived in semipermanent villages. Their dwellings, called "long houses," were made of poles and bark and accommodated several families.

French traders had purchased furs from the Indians of the St.

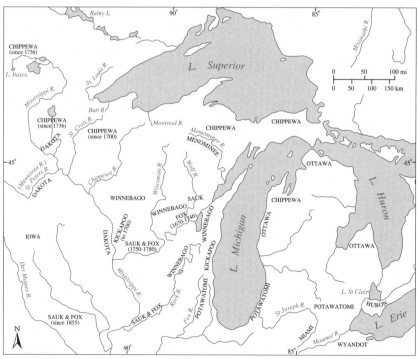

Indian tribes of the western Great Lakes.

Lawrence Valley for some years prior to the establishment of a permanent settlement. In 1603 the Company of One Hundred Associates, which had been granted a monopoly of the fur trade and charged with establishing the colony of New France, sent an exploring expedition to the St. Lawrence. Accompanying the expedition was 36-year-old Samuel de Champlain, who had acquired a reputation in France as a geographer and map maker. Champlain explored the St. Lawrence as far upriver as the Lachine Rapids and the point where the Ottawa River joins the St. Lawrence from the west. The St. Lawrence Valley was virtually trapped out by then, and the Ottawa River was the gateway to the fur-rich interior. From the headwaters of that stream, a short portage led to Lake Nipissing, which drained into Georgian Bay, an arm of Lake Huron. Although Champlain never made this passage, his Algonquin friends drew it out for him. He also learned that the people who sat astride this potential trade route were the Huron, one of the largest tribes in North America, who occupied most of the land between Lake Ontario and Lake Huron. The Hurons were blood enemies of the Iroquois, and the French were drawn inexorably into this tribal conflict. Champlain, who founded Quebec and became the first governor-general of New France, cast his lot with the Hurons in 1609 when he accompanied a party of them southward up the Richelieu River to the lake that bears his name. Near the point where Lake George joins Lake Champlain, the group encountered a war party of Iroquois. Champlain's men were armed with muskets, a weapon the Iroquois had never seen or heard. They fled in terror and never forgot the experience. For the next 90 years the Iroquois were the implacable enemies of the French. The fighting was not confined to the St. Lawrence Valley but spread across the entire Great Lakes region. The social disruption it occasioned would affect even the area that would become Wisconsin.

Champlain set the pattern for French relations with the Indians when he instituted a policy of sending young Frenchmen to live among the Indians, learning their language and culture. The first of these was Etienne Brule, who went to live with the Hurons in 1610. He adopted Indian dress and picked up the language quickly. Over the next 20 years he accompanied Huron expeditions that took him as far south as Chesapeake Bay and perhaps as far west as Lake Superior. The voyage to Lake Superior probably occurred in the years 1621-23 when he left a Huron village on Georgian Bay in a canoe with a single companion. Following the north shore of the bay, he entered the St. Mary's River (the French Sault Ste. Marie), pushed up through the rapids, and out onto the south shore of Lake Superior. He was the first white man to explore that lake and perhaps the first to visit Wisconsin. (The Brule River in northern Wisconsin was probably not named for him; its name stems instead from the French *bois brule*, or "burnt wood.") We really know little of Brule's adventures because, being in all likelihood illiterate, he never recorded them. We have only the recollections of French missionaries, who wrote down the tales that Brule gave them.

Champlain had brought the first missionaries to Quebec in 1615. A protege of Henry IV, the Protestant pretender who had converted to Catholicism in order to win the Crown (and thereby ended the religious conflict that had torn France apart for a quarter of a century), Champlain probably did not have deep religious convictions. He saw in the work of the missionaries something of strategic value to New France. Converted to Christianity and settled in communities dependent on the mission, the Indians would be tied culturally, as well as commercially, to New France. In actuality, the priests had little luck in making converts of the Indians, but they did posterity an important service by recording their own travels and those of the French explorers.

The first churchmen were Recollet priests (a puritanical suborder of the Franciscans) whom Champlain sent to live among the Hurons. Finding the challenge too vast for their small numbers, the Recollets in 1625 invited members of the Society of Jesus to join them. The Jesuits, a recently founded and intensely motivated order, spread across the Upper Great Lakes, establishing missions as far west as Green Bay and Madeline Island, and suffering in the process torture and death at the hands of Indians who rejected their message. The *Jesuit Relations*, published from 1632 until their suppression in 1673, is the most important single source of information on New

France in the 17th century.

Jean Nicolet was another of Champlain's "boys" sent to live with the Indians. He was about 20 years of age when he arrived in Canada in 1618 in the employ of a French trading company. For 10 years he lived among the Indian tribes along the fur-trading route, becoming fluent in their languages and accompanying their hunting parties to the most distant lakes and woods. Although he kept a journal of his experiences, it was lost in a canoe spill, and we have only the sketchy stories that he told to Jesuit missionaries. His most famous exploit was in 1634, the year before Champlain died. From the Hurons Champlain had learned of a people who resided on another large lake several hundred miles farther west and who spoke a strange language that the Hurons did not understand. Having seen the profits in the fur trade, the Hurons may have been eager to expand their source of supply.

Champlain's informants were telling him of the strange-speaking

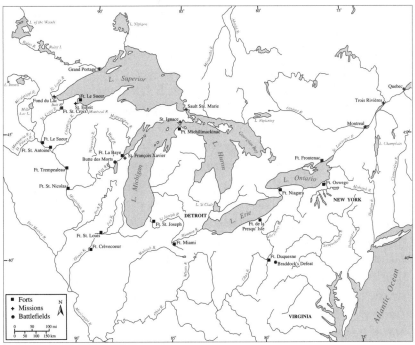

The French in the Great Lakes country.

Winnebagoes, who occupied the Fox River Valley of Wisconsin and the shores of Green Bay. Members of yet a third Indian language group, Siouxian, the Winnebago were known to their neighbors as "people of the dirty water," a reference, it is supposed, to the muddy waters of Lake Winnebago and the lower Fox River during the spring runoff. The Indian name that the French heard was recorded as "Ouinipeg" and was then given the French translation of Puant. Seizing upon the ambiguity of translation, Champlain decided that the Winnebagoes had once resided on salt water, and therefore they might be able to show the way to the Northwest Passage that led to the Pacific Ocean and thence to China. He sent Nicolet to explore the possibility.

In Quebec at the time, Nicolet packed carefully for every eventuality. Among the things he took along was a robe of damask silk, embroidered with birds and flowers of many colors, of the sort that Chinese mandarins were known to wear. He traversed the Ottawa River-Georgian Bay waterway, pausing to visit old friends in Huron villages along the way. Accompanied by seven Huron guides, he continued along the north shore of Lake Huron to the St. Mary's River. (The account in the *Jesuit Relations* is so vague on geography that it is uncertain whether he navigated the Sault Ste. Marie into Lake Superior or followed the Mackinac Straits into Lake Michigan, but we suppose the latter because the Huron guides must have known where the Winnebagoes lived.)

Upon entering Green Bay, Nicolet sent messages ahead to the Winnebago villages to ensure a proper reception. Having encountered nothing but fresh water and Indian tribes on his route, Nicolet was under no illusion that he had reached China. Nevertheless, he donned the silken robe and stepped majestically ashore with two pistols in his belt. Standing before a curious assemblage of several hundred Indians, he suddenly drew his pistols and fired into the air, causing the Indians to scatter in panic. Having demonstrated his divine power, Nicolet proceeded to demonstrate his friendly intentions by placing gifts on sticks in the ground. The Winnebago would remain fiercely loyal to France (or at least to Quebec, whoever held it) for the next 150 years. The short-term result of

Nicolet's visit was that the Winnebago became hunters and trappers in the fur business, and the Hurons became the middlemen.

Caught up in the fur trade with the Winnebago were their neighbors, the Menominee, whose villages were interspersed with the Winnebago settlements along the Fox River and Green Bay. Their language, though of the Algonquian family, had unique features due to their long residence in Wisconsin, and they required interpreters when they encountered the Algonquian tribes of Canada. More so than the Winnebago, who depended heavily on agriculture, the Menominee were hunters who held certain animals in reverence. (They believed mankind was descended from the bear.) The fur trade was more socially disruptive to them than to the Winnebago, as the tribe divided into roving bands devoted to trapping animals. That may have been a blessing in disguise, for the Menominee escaped much of the pestilence that swept away entire Winnebago villages toward the end of the 17th century.

▼

Growth of the Fur Trade

The fur trade blossomed in the decade after Nicolet's visit to Wisconsin. About 1640 French traders discovered the straits leading to Lake Superior and recruited the people living there. The French called them Saulteurs ("People of the Straits"); they called themselves Anishinabe ("Original Man"). Neighbors referred to them as the Ojibwa, probably a corruption of the Algonquian word *o-jib-e-weg*, meaning "those who make pictographs." A century later the English corrupted Ojibwa into Chippewa, and that is the name that went into the history books, although many modern members of the tribe prefer Ojibwa. The Ojibwa were a numerous tribe, which had migrated west from the St. Lawrence Valley in search of game. They were superb hunters and trappers (one band is alleged to have snared 1,200 moose on Manitoulin Island in the 1670s), and once they enlisted with the French the eastward flow of furs reached flood proportions. Montreal, founded in 1642 on an island near the mouth of the Ottawa River, became the center of the trade; three years later the French government renewed the monopoly of the

Hundred Associates.

Then, without warning, disaster struck. The Iroquois, who themselves acted as middlemen for Dutch traders in Albany, resented the diversion of furs to Montreal. They resented even more the prosperity of the Hurons, their ancient foes. In 1649 bands of the Iroquois confederacy, chiefly Mohawks and Senecas, fell on the defenseless Hurons. Although the Hurons fought well and even won a few encounters, the tribe eventually fled across Lake Michigan for safety. Some settled among the Winnebagoes; others scattered as far as the shores of Lake Superior. Other tribes, Potawatomi, Sauk and Fox, inhabiting the prairies south and east of Lake Michigan, migrated to Wisconsin about the same time, driven, it is supposed, by the warfare to the east.

Warfare with Illinois tribes and pestilence brought by the Europeans had reduced the Winnebago to a fraction of their former strength. The migrants took over the lands the Winnebago had once

The landfall of Jean Nicolet, 1634. Oil painting by Edwin W. Deming, 1904.

held. The Sauk settled along the Wisconsin River, the Fox occupied the valley that bears their name, and the Potawatomi set up villages along the shores of Lake Michigan. The Ojibwa, though under no pressure from the Iroquois, continued their westward movement along the south shore of Lake Superior. When the French established a post on Chequamegon Bay in 1692, traders estimated a population of 1,000 Ojibwa in the area.

The Iroquois, whose war parties threatened the very gates of Montreal, brought the Canadian fur trade to a virtual halt. Even the Jesuit missions on Lake Huron fell to the ferocious marauders. When the fur trade revived after the French arranged a truce with the Iroquois in 1654, it took on a new form. During the Iroquois war the only Frenchmen who had ventured into the west were independent traders, interlopers who had defied the governmental monopoly ever since the death of Champlain. Whereas the monopoly depended on Indian middlemen who brought the furs to Montreal, these carefree, tough young men, called *coureurs de bois*, traveled the western waters themselves to buy furs.

The chronicler of the *coureurs de bois* (other than Champlain, the first non-Jesuit chronicler of New France) was Pierre Esprit Radisson. Radisson's journals must be read with care because his manuscript, now lost, was translated into some of the most convoluted prose that has ever masqueraded as English. Yes, English—because by the time he set down his memoirs he had become frustrated with French monopolists and had offered his services to the English. He was probably not very literate in French either, and when he took quill in hand his mind bubbled with Indian terms. Nevertheless, it is possible to trace the routes he described with some precision. A citizen of no country, who betrayed his native France twice and his adopted England once, Radisson crossed the Atlantic 24 times, traversed Hudson Bay seven times, and paddled the length of the Great Lakes twice. His explorations added enormously to the European knowledge of the interior of North America, and he gave us the first contemporary description of Wisconsin.

The first journey described by Radisson was one in which he probably did not participate. It was led by his brother-in-law

Medard Chouart, a fur merchant who had bought himself a country estate on the edge of Three Rivers, the fur entrepot that ante-
dated Montreal, and styled himself, with the sardonic humor of a
coureur de bois, Sieur des Groseilliers ("Lord of the Gooseberries").
Taking advantage of the truce, Groseilliers led a trading party into
Lake Huron and returned with 50 canoes loaded with Indians and
furs. Radisson, in the meantime, had been captured by the Iroquois,
charmed them long enough to learn their language and customs,
and escaped.

In August 1659, Radisson and Groseilliers became partners in a
voyage to the westernmost lakes. They slipped out of Three Rivers
by night to avoid the authorities charged with enforcing the monopoly. Indians accompanied them all the way. They first attached themselves to a party of Hurons returning home after selling their furs in
Montreal. At Georgian Bay, the Hurons put them in the hands of the
Cree, lords of the spruce-filled wasteland between the Great Lakes
and Hudson Bay. The Cree, in turn, introduced them to the Menominees and Ojibwa who inhabited the south shore of Lake
Superior. Radisson's own familiarity with Indian customs and facility with languages must have smoothed these transferrals.

Despite storms that forced them ashore for days at a time, the
pair made its way along the south shore of Lake Superior. Radisson
recorded the principal landmarks in his journal—the Keweenaw
Peninsula, where the Indians showed him great nodules of copper
lying on the ground, the Ontonagon River with its sloughs of wild
rice and finally Chequamegon Bay. Their current guides (Ojibwa?
Huron? Fox?) left the two Frenchmen at the end of the bay and
went overland to their village to seek help in carrying the baggage.
Radisson and Groseilliers prudently built a small fort for themselves
and ringed it with snares to ward off intruders. They then went
hunting to prepare a feast for their companions. Local residents
turned up at the fortified hut periodically out of curiosity, but none
of them presented a threat. "We were Caesars," Radisson wrote,
"being nobody to contradict us."

After a fortnight the Indians returned with reinforcements,
most of them, apparently, women. The Frenchmen had cached half

their trading goods for future use; the women hoisted the remainder on their backs for the overland trek to the village. Radisson reimbursed their labor with a handful of trinkets, carefully keeping the amount low in order to avoid inflation. They reached the village after a march of four days through the woods. It was a beautiful country, Radisson observed, "with very few mountains [and] the woods clear."

The location of the village where Radisson and Groseilliers spent the winter of 1659-1660 has been the subject of much conjecture. The usual guess is Lac Court Oreilles, where travelers observed a large Ojibwa settlement a century later. Court Oreilles, however, is 70 miles south of Chequamegon Bay, and it is unlikely that a baggage-laden troop would have walked that far in four days. The access to Court Oreilles, moreover, was by water, via the Brule, St. Croix and Namekagon rivers. A better guess is Lake Namekagon, or perhaps nearby Lake Owen where there are extensive Indian mounds.

In any event, the Frenchmen were welcomed into the tribe and adopted by Indian families. During the winter the village split up to make hunting easier. Still, there was much hunger. Even with snowshoes ("racketts," Radisson called them), the Indians could not catch up with the deer, and other game were in hibernation. They were starving by the time an early spring ice storm put a crust on the snow that gave the Indians footing and hampered the deer.

Meanwhile, news of the white men had spread across the northwest, and in the spring the Sioux, neighbors to the west, sent a delegation to the village. The Sioux had seen European goods in the hands of Wisconsin Indians and were eager to become part of the fur trade. After days of feasting and trading trinkets for beaver skins, Radisson and Groseilliers agreed to visit the Sioux country. After a journey of seven days, they reached a colossal settlement of (so the Sioux claimed) 7,000 people, probably on Lake Mille Lacs in present-day Minnesota. The Sioux gave their guests 300 packs of beaver pelts, but the Frenchmen were able to carry only a few of them back. The return to Chequamegon Bay took 12 days. Radisson called them "easy journeys," which suggests they went by water, perhaps by way of the St. Croix and Brule rivers.

While with the Sioux, Radisson and Groseilliers promised to serve as intermediaries in ending a war between the Sioux and their traditional enemies, the Cree. A visit to the Cree involved a hazardous paddle across the western end of Lake Superior amid spring ice floes, but the Cree gave them a hearty welcome. Apparently they succeeded in their diplomatic mission (Radisson rarely records a failure at anything), and in addition swapped their remaining tools and trinkets for several boatloads of beaver pelts.

Radisson, who habitually extracted from the Indians all the geographical information they had, learned from the Cree of a great waterway to the northwest (Rainy Lake, the Lake of the Woods, Lake Winnipeg and the Nelson River) leading to a salt sea, which Radisson correctly surmised must be Hudson Bay. He instantly recognized the significance of this intelligence, for it promised a backdoor to the beaver country. A downriver trip to Hudson Bay would be easier and shorter than hauling furs all the way to Montreal, and it avoided the Iroquois menace. The vision of a Northwest Passage to Hudson Bay would dominate the rest of Radisson's life, and of many who came after him.

By August 1660 Radisson and Groseilliers were back in Montreal with 60 boatloads of furs paddled by friendly Indians. The market value came to a magnificent 140,000 livres (a livre was roughly equivalent to a Spanish dollar), and the shipment saved New France from economic collapse. The governor, however, refused to be grateful. A rigid functionary, he clapped the two adventurers in jail for having breached the monopoly and for leaving town without permission. Frustrated by the lack of enterprise on the part of the French government, Radisson and Groseilliers some years later deserted to England where their tales of a Northwest Passage resulted in the founding of the Hudson Bay Company in 1670.

▼

Jesuit Missionaries

The chaotic conditions in New France induced newly enthroned King Louis XIV to make it a royal colony in 1663. A succession of able administrators, Jean Talon and Count Frontenac, infused new vigor into the colony and revived the impulse to explore the interior of the continent. A French punitive expedition and the ravages of disease quieted the Iroquois and allowed the Algonquian tribes to renew their contacts with Montreal. As before, the missionaries were in the forefront of the French penetration of the wilderness. In 1663 the bishop in Montreal named a Jesuit, Claude Allouez, to be the vicar general of the whole interior of the continent. Allouez traversed Lake Superior and settled on Madeline Island at the mouth of Chequamegon Bay, where Christian Hurons had established a village. Naming the spot La Pointe, Father Allouez built a birchbark chapel to minister to the needs of any who would join his faith. Six years later another Jesuit, Father Jacques Marquette, arrived at La Pointe, and Allouez transferred his missionary endeavors to Green Bay and the Fox River Valley. In the winter of 1671-1672 he established the first permanent mission house in the region, St. Francis Xavier at De Pere.

The Jesuits had very little success in converting Indians, who found Christian theology perplexing and the Jesuits' behavioral regimen too rigorous. Most woodland Indians believed in a supreme being, benevolent and the creator of life. However, this being did not participate directly in the affairs of the earth; it worked instead through a host of subordinate deities, which controlled the weather, lured game to hunters, and affected the health of families. Before undertaking a journey, an Indian would propitiate the god of the waters; if he failed on the hunt, he attributed it to the subdeity that governed such things. His wife made an offering to the rice god before gathering the harvest. There were also evil spirits that had to be avoided. The Ojibwa lived in terror of the Windigo, a man-eating giant who lurked in the winter woods. Caves, waterfalls and other curious features of the landscape, the obvious abodes of the spirits, were both avoided and venerated. The religion of the woodland Indians was thus a practical matter, based on satisfying basic economic needs and preserving life and health. Christianity, on the other hand, demanded an esoteric commitment to a prophet long since dead with little or no immediate reward for the convert.

Conversion to Christianity also involved a substantial change in the Indians' living arrangements. The priests demanded that converts settle in villages near the missions, no doubt fearing that they would revert to heathenism if they were allowed to return to the woods. Some Indian men found this advantageous because it placed them near the source of European goods and gave them a better market for their furs. Both clergy and government officials showered favors on male converts, which increased their social status.

The impact on women, on the other hand, was quite the opposite. Women had an important role in woodland society. They controlled the distribution of food and selected campsites. They snared small animals, gathered nuts and berries, and harvested wild rice. When a male returned with a deer or bear, his wife took charge of the meat, cut it up, and determined which parts would be distributed to friends or relatives. The wife also processed the hide, turning it into clothing, bedding or moccasins. She fashioned the animal's bones into needles, ladles and other household implements. The fur trade, and particularly residence in a mission village, threatened all this. The trade gave the Indians access to European clothing and tools. The Indian woman's role was reduced to scraping furs in preparation for sale. Instead of making key decisions and producing satisfying end-products, she became a mere auxiliary in a complex commercial enterprise.

Conversion adversely affected Indian women in another way. The priests insisted that converts remain monogamous. The woodland tribes, like most primitive peoples, practiced polygamy. For many women it was a matter of survival. Because of chronic warfare, there was a sexual imbalance in every tribe. Multiple marriage was the only way some women could gain the security of family life and the prospect of children, who were essential for care in old age. Because men were gone much of the time, at war or the hunt, women formed a sort of sisterhood of mutual support; often wives were blood sisters in fact. Marriage among Indians was a simple ceremony, and divorce was equally easy. This too benefited women because it allowed them to control their lives and fortunes. Yet divorce was another practice disallowed by the Roman Catholic priests.

Both Indian men and the Jesuit missionaries noted the resistance of women to Christianity. Father Louis Andre at Green Bay managed to convert a few women, but he never really trusted them. When his cabin burned mysteriously in 1672, he was certain that women had put it to the torch because "the old women especially blamed me greatly because I said that the evil spirit should be neither obeyed nor feared." Female resistance was only one of the factors in the failure of the Jesuit missionary endeavor. Nevertheless, despite the courage and zeal of the Jesuit fathers themselves, it must be accounted a failure. By the end of the century, missionary work in the Upper Great Lakes had virtually come to a halt.

▼

Pushing West

Before they departed, the Jesuits made one final contribution to the development of both Wisconsin and New France—the discovery and exploration of the "Great River," about which rumors had abounded ever since the time of Nicolet. At Chequamegon Bay Indians told Allouez about the "Messipi" ("sepi" was the word for river in several Algonquian languages). What the French did not

La Pointe, Madeline Island in Chequamegon Bay. Photographed in 1898 by S.W. Bailey of Ashland. The large building on the left is a mission established in 1830.

know was whether it flowed north to Hudson Bay or south to either the Gulf of Mexico or the Pacific. In the summer of 1672 Jean Talon commissioned Louis Joliet, mapmaker, explorer and fur trader, to search for the "Sea of the South and for the Great River which the Indians called Michissipi." France's new governor, Count Frontenac, arrived soon thereafter and confirmed the appointment. Frontenac, who had secret orders to curb the activities of the Jesuits, was probably delighted that Talon had selected a layman. However, when the Jesuit brotherhood insisted on participating, the governor diplomatically added Father Jacques Marquette. A Sioux war party had chased Marquette out of his mission on Mackinac Island, and Joliet found him in the spring of 1673 conducting services in a rude log cabin at St. Ignace on the north shore of Lake Michigan.

On May 17 the pair embarked with five men in two canoes. They paddled along the western shore of Green Bay, ascended the Fox River, skirted the western shore of Lake Winnebago, and pushed farther up the Fox to an Indian village near present-day Berlin that Father Allouez had visited several years before. This was the western limit of French geographical knowledge. Two Indians from the village guided them through the tangle of wild rice in the upper part of the stream and helped them carry their canoes over the two-mile portage to a much grander river. The Indians had a name for this stream, which Joliet recorded as Miskonsing and Marquette remembered as Meskousing. We know it today as the Wisconsin. Students of Indian languages have puzzled over its meaning without reaching any conclusion. The trip down the Wisconsin River went smoothly, and on the 17th of June the explorers paddled out onto the Mississippi. The strategic importance of their venture, from the standpoint of French diplomacy, was the discovery that the river flowed south toward the Spanish settlements, rather than north toward the British outposts on Hudson Bay. Marquette and Joliet journeyed as far as the mouth of the Arkansas River, where they encountered Indians with European goods. Not wishing to fall into the hands of the Spanish, the explorers turned back, returning to Lake Michigan by way of the Illinois River and the Chicago-Des Plaines portage. It was this route, via the Illinois

River, that Robert Cavelier, Sieur de LaSalle, followed when he traced the Mississippi all the way to its mouth (1679-1682) and claimed for France all the lands that it drained, naming this continental heartland after the French king, Louisiana.

The discovery of the Fox-Wisconsin waterway opened the eyes of the French to the potential for expanding the fur trade west of the Mississippi. This was the domain of the mighty Sioux (or Dakota, as they called themselves), who had so far remained outside the circle of French influence. The Sioux were a puzzle; for a decade and more they had menaced French missions as far east as Mackinac while showing an interest in French trading goods. They were fast making enemies of the Ojibwa and other Wisconsin tribes by attacking trappers and traders.

In the summer of 1678 a group of Montreal fur merchants organized an expedition to open trade with the Sioux. To lead it they chose Daniel Greysolon, Sieur du Lhut or Duluth, as his name has come down to us. Brave and enterprising, a member of the lesser nobility, Duluth had come to Canada in 1672 and settled in Montreal, where his uncle was a successful merchant. In the fall of 1678 he traveled with seven companions to the Sault Ste. Marie, where he made the acquaintance of the Ojibwa. Like other successful French explorers, Duluth had a facility for language and a sensitivity to Indian ways. The following spring, "fearing not death, only cowardice and dishonor," he led his party to the western end of Lake Superior. At a meeting near the site of the city that bears his name, he negotiated a peace agreement between the Sioux and the Ojibwa. He then traveled on to the Sioux village at Lake Mille Lacs in present-day Minnesota. He sent three of his men to venture farther to the west, and Duluth himself returned to his base on the shore of Lake Superior.

His three adventurers returned the following spring, having journeyed probably as far as the Dakota plains. Duluth later wrote that the trio had "brought me some ... salt, having reported to me that the savages had told them that it was only twenty days' journey from where they were to the discovery of the great lake whose water is not good to drink." Since the Indian informants were no doubt talking of travel by horseback, they could well have been referring to the Great Salt Lake. Duluth, of course, assumed they were talking about the Pacific Ocean. Before leaving Montreal, his imagination had been fired by the thought of reaching the Western Sea; he now resolved to find it.

Unfortunately, his Indian friends failed to tell Duluth about the passage that Radisson had found leading from the northwest shore of Lake Superior to westward flowing rivers that drained into the Lake of the Woods, Lake Winnipeg and ultimately Hudson Bay. It was the closest approximation of a Northwest Passage that the continent would have. Duluth instead looked for a passageway on the south shore of Lake Superior and came upon the Brule River a few miles east of his base. Portaging around the foaming rapids through which the stream drops precipitously into Lake Superior, Duluth came upon a smooth-flowing stream that led him far into the interior. From the headwaters of the Brule he portaged over to the St. Croix River and followed that "through all its foaming rapids" to its junction with the Mississippi. Though not the Northwest Passage, Duluth had discovered another water route across Wisconsin between the Great Lakes and the Mississippi. At the river junction Duluth rescued a Jesuit priest who had strayed from LaSalle's expedition and been captured by the Sioux. Abandoning for the present his plans for exploration, Duluth returned east by the Fox-Wisconsin waterway.

▼

The End of French Rule

The final 80 years of French rule, which ended with the surrender of Montreal to the British in 1760, witnessed almost constant warfare, much of it in Wisconsin. The struggle with the Iroquois broke out again in 1680. A string of French defeats climaxed with the Lachine Massacre in 1688 at the outskirts of Montreal. Taking advantage of French weakness, an English fleet of 11 trading canoes reached Mackinac by way of lakes Erie and Huron, thus breaking the French monopoly on the fur trade of the upper lakes. Although French military power in Wisconsin was nil, Duluth and Nicholas

Perrot, a Green Bay trader, managed to keep the Wisconsin tribes at peace, and some war parties even traveled east to help the French in the St. Lawrence basin. The war finally ended with a virtual surrender by the exhausted Iroquois in 1700.

That peace brought no rest for the French in Wisconsin, however. The Fox Indians, having been pushed out of the northwestern rivers by the Ojibwa, concentrated their villages on the lower Fox River. They thus stood astride the gateway to the West and the trans-Mississippi fur trade. Although they were inclined to forgive the Ojibwa, the Fox were mortal enemies of the Sioux. They resented the French trade with the Sioux and worried lest the Sioux acquire French firearms. As a result, they blocked the waterway and cut off all canoe passage to the West. From 1701 to 1713 the French were locked in a European war with Britain and Austria, a contest that ended with France's cession to Britain of Newfoundland, Nova Scotia and Hudson Bay. Taking advantage of France's preoccupation

Ojibwa women making maple sugar. From a lithograph in Henry Rowe Schoolcraft's Indian Tribes of the United States *(1851).*

with Europe, the Fox formed a military alliance with the Sauk, Kickapoo and Mascoutin. Until 1715 no Frenchman or French-allied Indian was safe in the Wisconsin woods. In that year the French sent an expedition of 800 soldiers, equipped with mortars and small cannon, to Green Bay. The Indians surrendered and were given generous terms that required them only to pay the cost of the war by trapping beaver.

In 1717 the French built a solid fort at La Baye (as they called Green Bay), and the following year they erected a fort at La Pointe on Madeline Island. The French show of strength caused new concern among the Indians and won the Fox new allies, even among their former enemies, the Sioux and Iowa tribes west of the Mississippi. Kiala, the dynamic leader of the Fox, formed an alliance with these western tribes and obtained additional support from the Sauk, Kickapoo and Winnebago, who had now recovered their numbers by intermarrying with their neighbors. The coalition wrested control of Illinois from the French and closed the Chicago-Des Plaines portage to the Illinois River. In 1728 the French sent another massive expedition into the Fox River Valley. The Indians evapo-

Ojibwa women harvesting rice. From a lithograph in Henry Rowe Schoolcraft's Indian Tribes of the United States *(1851).*

rated into the woods, and the French commander had to content himself with burning their villages. He then withdrew, confessing his frustration by destroying the fort at La Baye.

The implacable Fox refused to sue for peace, and the war dragged on year after year. In 1733 both the French and the Fox suffered heavy losses in a pitched battle at Little Buttes des Morts, on the Wolf River west of Lake Winnebago. The following year a French expedition went as far as Iowa without much military success, but the constant fighting totally disrupted the Indian economy. The Fox confederacy broke up, and in 1737 the French and Indians at last reached a peace that allowed the Fox to return to their Green Bay habitat.

The chief beneficiaries of the Fox wars were the Ojibwa. Taking advantage of Fox weakness, the Ojibwa drove them out of the rivers draining into Lake Superior and pushed their own frontier to the south and west of the lake. About 1745 they set up their first permanent village in the interior on the shores of Lac Court Oreilles, one of the headwaters of the Chippewa River. Attracted by the lucrative fur trade west of the Grand Portage, the Chippewa set up pioneer settlements at Rainy Lake and the Lake of the Woods. This westward movement brought them head to head with the Sioux, with whom they had already had sporadic conflict. A linguistic and cultural gap separated the two peoples; territorial disputes quickly escalated into open warfare. Like the classic Hundred Years War of the Middle Ages, the fighting continued off and on for a century. It did not cease until well after a majority of the Sioux moved out of the woodlands and onto the Great Plains.

Because the fighting was so prolonged and the rivalry so bitter, this tribal "border war" caught the attention of traders and missionaries, and they have left us a fairly graphic picture of the Indian style of warfare. There was neither a prevailing strategy nor broad participation. One village fought another, often over hunting grounds or wild rice marshes, while villages on either side remained at truce. A warrior commonly invited other men to join a war party that he would lead. Young men were often introduced to warfare by their uncles, who, in turn, were responsible for their survival. Upon completion of a raid, the war party was dissolved. As late as the 19th century an eyewitness to a battle reported that firearms and ammunition were so scarce that guns were used for signal purposes only and that both sides waged war with club in one hand and knife in the other. Although numbers were small, the loss of life was sometimes very high. One very successful Ojibwa raid returned with 335 Dakota scalps.

A new war with Britain, known to the seaboard colonists as King George's War (1744-1748), further weakened the French and their hold on Wisconsin. A British blockade prevented the import of trading goods and drove prices at Mackinac up by as much as 150 percent. The Indians by then had become increasingly critical of French goods. British manufactures, trickling into the western lakes from Albany, were better made and cheaper.

The next conflict, known in America as the French and Indian War (1756-1763), terminated the French empire in North America. Most Wisconsin tribes no doubt viewed the fate of the French with indifference, but one young soldier insisted that Wisconsin participate in the war. His name was Charles Langlade, a half-breed who had settled at La Baye and is regarded as Wisconsin's first year-round white resident. Langlade joined the French army, receiving a commission as an ensign in 1755 and promoted to lieutenant in 1760. In 1755 Langlade commanded a force of Wisconsin Indians, most of them Ojibwas, in Braddock's defeat in the Monongahela Valley in western Pennsylvania. Four years later Langlade's Indians were in the Battle of the Plains of Abraham outside Quebec. Langlade and his band were returning to Mackinac in September 1760 when they received news of the surrender of Montreal and with it French Canada. A year later a British force arrived at Fort Mackinac to receive Lieutenant Langlade's surrender. The victors then moved on to Fort La Baye, which had long since been abandoned by the French. Not even a fur trader was to be found in the village.

By the terms of the peace treaty that formally ended the war in 1763, France ceded Canada to Britain, as well as the portion of Louisiana that lay east of the Mississippi. Louisiana west of the Mississippi it ceded to Spain. For Wisconsin, destruction of the

French empire in North America meant only a change of masters. The British, headquartered in Quebec and Montreal, now took over the fur trade and hence the destiny of Wisconsin's inhabitants. The Indians, completely dependent on European goods, had all but lost the arts of wilderness survival. A traveler along the shores of Lake Superior a few years later found the Indians ragged and starving. The war had cut off their supply of goods, and they had lost the skill of hunting with bow and arrow. This reliance upon British traders continued for many years after the Revolution and American independence, and it dictated the role of Wisconsin in world events for decades to come.

▼

Travelers' Guide

Indians and Fur Traders

Chippewa Valley Museum, Carson Park, Eau Claire; (715) 834-7871. Exhibit traces the history of the Ojibwa Indians.

Heritage Hill State Park, 2640 S. Webster Ave., Green Bay; (414) 448-5150. Twenty-five historic buildings, including a replica of a Jesuit missionary's bark chapel and a 1762 fur trader's cabin.

Lac du Flambeau Chippewa Museum and Cultural Center, County D off Highway 47 near Lac du Flambeau; (715) 588-3333. Four-seasons diorama, traditional arts and crafts, dugout canoe, fur-trading post, world-record sturgeon.

Madeline Island Historical Museum, one block from the ferry landing, La Pointe; (715) 747-2415. Exhibits on the Chippewa, fur traders and missionaries who visited and lived in this important Lake Superior settlement.

Milwaukee Public Museum, 800 W. Wells St., Milwaukee; (414) 278-2702. Permanent exhibit on Wisconsin Indians.

Oshkosh Public Museum, 1331 Algoma Blvd., Oshkosh; (414) 424-4730. Exhibits on the local fur trade and Indian tribes.

Northern Wisconsin Interpretive Center, 400 Third Ave. West,

Ashland; (715) 682-6600. Exhibits on area history, including the fur trade.

St. Croix National Scenic Riverway. A pristine river corridor that looks much as it did when Indians and traders paddled its waters. Staff at information centers in St. Croix Falls (P.O. Box 708, St. Croix Falls, WI 54024; 715-483-3284) and on Highway 63 in Trego can provide information on canoeing, camping and picnicking facilities. The centers also contain displays on the river's history.

State Historical Museum, 30 N. Carroll St., Madison; (608) 264-6555. Permanent exhibit on Wisconsin Indian life.

Villa Louis, 521 Villa Louis Rd., Prairie du Chien; (608) 326-2721. Victorian mansion, and State Historic Site, built by the descendents of Hercules Dousman, who made his fortune in the fur trade. Includes the Fur Trade Museum.

Chapter 3

FROM WILDERNESS TO STATEHOOD

One of the heroes of the French and Indian War was Massachusetts-born Robert Rogers, who organized a company of New Englanders who called themselves Rogers' Rangers. The Rangers earned a reputation for courage and endurance in the fighting around Lake Champlain. They accompanied General James Wolfe's expedition to Quebec in 1759, and they assisted Lord Jeffrey Amherst's conquest of Montreal in 1760. After the war Rogers journeyed to England seeking authorization for an expedition to look for the long-sought water route from the western tip of Lake Superior to the Pacific Ocean. He was given instead command of the fort at the straits of Mackinac, but that did not dim his hopes of finding the fabled Northwest Passage. His first move was to dispatch one of his ex-Rangers, Captain Jonathan Carver, to Wisconsin with rather vague instructions to invite the Indians to a grand council, where, presumably, they would be asked to swear loyalty to Great Britain.

▼

Travels of Jonathan Carver

Carver paddled the Fox-Wisconsin waterway and arrived in Prairie du Chien in October 1766. Although Carver's was the first Anglo-American expedition to the Mississippi, it might have been soon forgotten had not Carver published his journal in England a decade later. Entitled *Travels Through the Interior Parts of North America in 1766, 1767, and 1768,* it was the first description of the Upper Great Lakes by an Englishman. Although heavily dependent on available French accounts (British travelers in America would crib from one another for the next century), Carver's journal was widely read, eventually going through 40 editions. From its pages we can glean the first detailed description of the landscape and people of western Wisconsin.

Carver was delighted with the site the French had named Prairie du Chien, which a contemporary English fur trader translated as "Planes of the Dogs." Although the French had earlier erected a fort near the junction of the Wisconsin River and the Mississippi, Carver made no mention of French traders or villagers, perhaps because he arrived in the off season. Instead he found a Fox Indian village of about 300 families, their dwellings "well built after the Indian manner" (i.e., long houses of saplings covered with bark). All of the Wisconsin Indian tribes gathered in agricultural villages in the summer, while dispersing for the hunt in the winter. Carver considered the Fox village at Prairie du Chien "the largest and best built Indian town" he ever saw, and he was struck by its "regular and spacious streets." He accounted it, on the whole, "one of the most delightsome settlements I saw during my travels." He also noted "many horses of a good size and shape," which suggests that the Fox had trading contacts with the mounted Indians of the Great Plains.

After spending the winter with the Sioux on the Minnesota River, Carver returned to Prairie du Chien where he met two emissaries from Mackinac. By this time Rogers' plans had matured, and he had new instructions for Carver. Together with Rogers' soldiers, he was to move north to Lake Superior, where supplies would await them for an overland trip to the Pacific Ocean, encountering on the way, they hoped, a passage to Hudson Bay. In May 1767 the threesome, with two French interpreters, an Ojibwa guide and assorted paddlers, ascended the Mississippi to the mouth of the Chippewa River. Their guide led them up that stream in order to avoid the Sioux who inhabited the upper Mississippi. Carver was much impressed with the lower part of the Chippewa Valley. "Here I found very good land and very pleasant country," he wrote, "one might travel all day and only see now and then a small pleasant Grove of Oak and Walnut. [T]his Country is covered with Grass which affords excellent pasturage for the Buffaloe which here are very Plenty. Could see them at a Distance under the shady Oaks like Cattle in a Pasture. Here is a great Plenty of Elk the Largest that Ever I had seen." Above the falls of the Chippewa, however, his party came upon "a Most Dreary Wilderness of Trees or timber of all sorts but Principally Birch." Near the headwaters of the Chippewa a tributary (the Couderay River today) led the party to Lac Court d'Oreilles and an Ojibwa village on its western shore. Carver described it thus: "This town stands on a neck of land between two lakes [the second lake is known as Grindstone today] on each side of a small channel about 4 rods wide and very rapid which joins them and contains about fifteen houses and seventy warriors."

Carver's party obtained new guides at the Court d'Oreilles village, who led them across a short portage to Windigo Lake. From its western end, a mile-long jaunt overland brought them to the Namekagon River. They then proceeded by way of the St. Croix and the Brule to Lake Superior. Carver noted that the countryside was hilly and thickly covered with woods. "In the heads of the St. Croix and Chippeway Rivers are exceeding fine sturgeon," he recorded. "All the wilderness between the Mississippi and Lake Superior is called by the Indians the Moschettoe country, and I thought it most justly named; for, it being then their season, I never saw or felt so many of those insects in my life." The expedition arrived at Grand Portage on July 19 and found no cache of provisions. After they had waited there for three weeks, a messenger arrived with letters from Rogers informing his agents that he could not send supplies. Lacking wherewithal to provision themselves, the explorers returned to the fort at Mackinac. By the time they arrived, Rogers was in jail awaiting a court martial for diverting government funds and disobeying orders. "Here," wrote Carver sadly, "ends this attemp to find out a Northwest Passage." Rogers returned to England, and despite his shoddy treatment at the hands of the British, he fought with the British army in the American Revolution. He died in obscurity in England in 1795.

English authorities in Montreal quickly revived the fur trade after the French and Indian War, though most of the traders in the western lakes continued to be French *coureurs de bois*. By the 1770s the beaver had nearly vanished in Wisconsin, and the hunt for furs had moved west of the Mississippi. Although it had no military post, provisioner or year-round white inhabitants, Prairie du Chien was a major rendezvous point because of its strategic location at the Fox-Wisconsin and Mississippi crossroads. Peter Pond, a Connecticut Yankee who began trading on the Minnesota River in 1773, described a rendezvous at the "Planes of the Dogs" in the following spring. Boats had come up the Mississippi with trading goods from as far as New Orleans. A flotilla of 130 canoes, each capable of carrying 600 to 800 pounds, had come from Mackinac. He could not guess the number of Indians who had come to trade, but he estimated their camp along the river at a mile and a half in length. Traders sent 1,500 packs of furs weighing 100 pounds each back to Mackinac. "After all the Bisness Was Dun," wrote Pond, "and People Began to Groe tirde of Sport, they Began to Draw of[f] for thate Different Departments and Prepared for Insewing Winter."

The American Revolution, which broke out the following year, had almost no impact on the woodlands west of Lake Michigan. The Indians were content with their relations with the British, who had adopted the French practice of providing them with gifts and ammunition. They had, moreover, no reason to side with the Americans, whose settlement of Kentucky provoked conflict with the Ohio Valley tribes. The French traders likewise profited from the British connection, and they had no cultural or economic ties with the American colonists. The only military authority in the region was in the person of Charles Langlade who had settled at La Baye (renamed Green Bay by the British because spring came earlier there than at Mackinac) and had been made an officer in the British Indian service. In 1776 Langlade led a contingent of Wisconsin Indians to serve with the British in the St. Lawrence Valley, and the following year he accompanied General John

Burgoyne on his disastrous invasion of upstate New York. Burgoyne's surrender at Saratoga cooled the ardor of the Fox Valley Indians, however, and George Rogers Clark's spectacular capture of the British outpost at Vincennes, Indiana, in February 1779 brought the Indians of southern Wisconsin over to the American side. It was a momentary sympathy, however, for the westward movement of white settlers after the war awakened the Indians to a new threat to their lands and culture. In desperation they once again embraced the British lion.

▼

Settlement Begins

In the course of the Revolution several French traders, who had connections with Spanish merchants in St. Louis, settled in Prairie du Chien. In 1781 three of them purchased from the Fox Indians a nine-mile-square tract on the flats ("prairie") near the mouth of the Wisconsin River. The five original residents of the settlement were all French Catholics. Two had come from farther down the Mississippi; three were from Canada. All were fur traders, and all had Indian wives. Twenty years later, in 1800, a few British-Canadians had joined the village, but there was only one known American, an independent trader.

In the years after the Revolution the American states ceded to the Continental Congress the western land claims that had been part of the original royal grants. Congress thus inherited a public domain bounded by the Ohio and Mississippi rivers and the Great Lakes. In 1785 it passed an ordinance providing for the survey and sale of this inland empire. Beginning at the point where the Ohio River emerges from Pennsylvania, the ordinance authorized the survey of a series of longitudinal and latitudinal lines six miles apart, creating a grid of squares six miles on a side, on which Congress conferred the New England name "towns." Each town contained 36 mile-square sections (640 acres), which could be subdivided into farm-sized plots of 320 or 160 acres. The ordinance thus provided for an orderly disposition of the West. The price of order, however, was a snail's pace. By 1800 only the southeastern corner of Ohio was surveyed, and no significant amount of Wisconsin came under the surveyor's stake until the 1830s. The result was that pioneers pressed ahead of the surveyors, "squatting" on the land before it came up for sale, and Congress had to pass a succession of laws protecting the rights of squatters against land jobbers who made a business out of the government land office.

Two years later Congress passed another ordinance, providing this time for the government of its western "colony." The Northwest Ordinance of 1787 envisioned ultimate statehood for the Northwest after an interim period of "colonial" rule, limiting the number of states to between three and five. (Five was the number ultimately formed.) It then set up a series of steps by which a wilderness could evolve into a state on a par with the original 13. In the initial territorial stage Congress (after 1789, the president) named the governor and judges, although male voters could elect a legislature when the population reached a certain number. After the population reached 60,000 (the size of Delaware, smallest of the original 13 states), the territory could hold a convention, draft a state constitution, and petition Congress for admission to the Union. The first of the five states carved out of the Northwest Territory, Ohio, joined the Union

The village of Portage and Fort Winnebago in 1831.

in 1803 and the last, Wisconsin, joined in 1848.

Like the Ordinance of 1785, the act of 1787 had little immediate impact on Wisconsin, which found itself an appendage successively to the Indiana, Illinois and Michigan territories. In the meantime, the ordinances encouraged a steady advance of white settlement that increasingly threatened the possessions and the culture of the French and Indian inhabitants. The movement of white pioneers north of the Ohio River in the 1790s precipitated a series of bloody clashes that culminated in the total defeat of the Indians at the Battle of Fallen Timbers in 1794. The following year, in a gigantic conference at Greenville, Ohio, to which the Wisconsin tribes sent delegates, the United States Army forced the Indians to cede all but the northwest corner of Ohio. The boundary drawn at Greenville, running from Lake Erie to the Ohio River, was supposed to be permanent, but it proved exceedingly fragile. Over the next decade the federal government aggressively pried half of Indiana and two-thirds of Illinois from the hands of the Indians, usually with bribes of money and whiskey. The specter of fence and plow reached Wisconsin's woodlands in 1804 when a group of subordinate Sauk chiefs went to St. Louis to secure the release of one of their tribesmen who had been arrested on a charge of murdering a white citizen. While there, they were induced to sign away their rights to lands along the Mississippi between the Illinois and Wisconsin rivers in return for an annual payment of $1,000.

▼

Indian Resistance

In the first decade of the 19th century, Tecumseh, a charismatic Shawnee whose people had been pushed out of Ohio by the advance of white settlement, sought to form an alliance of the northwestern tribes to resist any further land cessions. The glue that held together Tecumseh's confederacy was the messianic appeal of his brother, the Prophet, who preached a doctrine that the red man would ultimately triumph if he rejected the sins of white civilization, notably liquor and gambling. The Prophet's voice was heard across Wisconsin, even to the shores of Lake Superior, where the

Chippewa threw their medicine pouches into the water and embraced the new religion. Traders who in desperation offered the Indians free whiskey found themselves scornfully rejected.

Although Tecumseh's alliance was purely defensive, William Henry Harrison, governor of the Indiana Territory, correctly saw it as a serious obstruction to the advance of the frontier. In November 1811, taking advantage of Tecumseh's absence on a recruiting trip in Missouri, Harrison struck at the Prophet's Town on Tippecanoe Creek in northern Indiana. The Prophet's followers fought hard for a couple of hours and then fled into the woods. The Battle of Tippecanoe was, in a sense, the first shot of the War of 1812, for Harrison's army found crates of guns in the Indian village that provided hard evidence of British involvement in western affairs. For years Congress had suffered the humiliation of Britain's invasion of American rights on the high seas; British intrigue among American Indians was more than it could bear. Congress declared war in June 1812.

Tecumseh promptly allied himself with the British, and the Wisconsin tribes joined him en masse. While the French and Indian inhabitants of the territory had been somewhat ambiguous during the American Revolution, there was total unanimity during the War of 1812. Not a pro-American voice could be heard anywhere in the land west of Lake Michigan. Within a month after the declaration of war, a force of Canadians, together with several hundred Sioux, Winnebagoes and Menominees, appeared outside the fort at Mackinac. The commander, who had not yet heard that a war had begun, surrendered without firing a shot. After learning of the fall of Fort Mackinac, the American general commanding in Detroit ordered the evacuation of Fort Dearborn at the foot of Lake Michigan. The Sauk and Fox, joined by other southern Wisconsin Indians, fell on the retreating garrison and massacred it. By August 1812 Tecumseh commanded a force of 1,000 warriors, and the commander at Detroit, fearful of another massacre, surrendered to an inferior British-Canadian force that had never stepped out of Canada. With the surrender of Detroit, everything north and west of Fort Wayne, Indiana, was in Indian hands. The handful of

Americans living at Prairie du Chien fled down the Mississippi, and the Winnebagoes plundered their property.

In the summer of 1813 General Harrison mounted a counterattack to recover Detroit, and once more Wisconsin Indians answered the call to arms. Robert Dickson, a Canadian fur trader, gathered an uncounted number at Green Bay, but a shortage of canoes allowed him to take only 600 on to Mackinac. A third of these were Menominee led by chief Tomah; the remainder were Winnebago and Sioux. Converging on Detroit from the south was a party of Sauk Indians, 500 strong, led by a rather youthful chief named Black Hawk.

With the aid of an American naval victory, Harrison crossed Lake Erie and invaded upper Canada. The British commander, an utter coward, evacuated Detroit and retreated eastward. Tecumseh finally forced him to make a stand at the Thames River, some 50 miles east of Detroit. The Battle of the Thames in October 1813, fought mostly by the Indians while the British commander sat in his carriage prepared to flee to Montreal, was an overwhelming American victory. Tecumseh was killed, Indian morale devastated. The battle, together with Andrew Jackson's victory at the Horseshoe Bend in Alabama the following spring, ended any further organized Indian resistance east of the Mississippi River. The treaty of peace, signed on Christmas Eve 1814, ended Britain's domination of Wisconsin.

▼

Black Hawk's War
and the Ceding of Indian Lands

Since 1809 Wisconsin had been governed as part of the Illinois Territory, but when Illinois became a state in 1818 the land between Lake Michigan and the Mississippi was attached to the Michigan Territory. There were still only two white settlements, Green Bay and Prairie du Chien, but the federal government had built a fort at each: Fort Howard at Green Bay and Fort Crawford at Prairie du Chien. The military presence gave each a certain status, not to say added income.

The economy was still based on furs, but the British no longer controlled the trade. Indeed, the American government after the war explicitly banned British-Canadians from trading on American soil.

The new force in the fur trade was John Jacob Astor, a self-made German immigrant, who had formed the nation's first "big business" corporation, the American Fur Company, in 1808. Unable to compete with the British in the Great Lakes trade before the war, Astor had concentrated on the Missouri River Valley. With the return of peace, he looked hungrily at the fur-bearing forests west of Lake Michigan. Unfortunately the beaver had long since been trapped out, and Astor's agents had to settle for less valuable pelts, such as fox, bear and raccoon. The returns on these were so puny that Astor soon lost interest, and by the end of the decade he had turned to speculating in Wisconsin lands.

Speculation in rising land prices had become a popular enterprise because of rapid population growth. The elimination of Tecumseh's confederacy opened the Northwest to white pioneers. Within six years after the end of the war Indiana, Illinois and Missouri had achieved statehood, and migrants were spilling over into Wisconsin and Iowa. The federal census of 1820 reported 651 civilians west of Lake Michigan and 804 soldiers. A decade later the region had more than 3,000 inhabitants, and when the Wisconsin Territory was established in 1836, a census revealed a population of 11,683.

In the 1820s the Indians still owned all of Wisconsin, except for pinpoints of white settlement at Green Bay, Milwaukee, Portage and Prairie du Chien. The arrival of land-hungry pioneers, however, put pressure on the government to secure Indian land cessions. When lead was discovered in the southwest near the Illinois border, whites invaded Indian lands to stake claims. In 1827 outraged Winnebagoes murdered settlers who had encroached on their lands, and this gave the government an excuse to act. Militia converged on the hapless Winnebago from Green Bay, Fort Snelling (St. Paul) and even Illinois. The Army built a new fort (Fort Winnebago) at the Fox-Wisconsin portage. In the summer of 1829 American commissioners summoned representatives from all the Wisconsin and Illinois tribes to a conference at Prairie du Chien. After intense negotiations, some of the Indians were persuaded to sell their lands. The big losers were the Sauk and Fox, who had offended no one, but who happened to stand in the way of the advancing mining frontier. They were forced to sell their remaining holdings between the Wisconsin River and the Rock River of Illinois. The Winnebago were next. They yielded any claims they might have to this same territory, as well as lands along the Wisconsin River as far up as the great portage. These forced cessions set the stage for the last Indian conflict east of the Mississippi, "Black Hawk's war."

For more than a century the Sauk and Fox tribes had been retreating before the unrelenting pressure of the white frontier, resisting at times, most recently when they sided with Tecumseh and the British in the War of 1812. By the 1820s they had been pushed into the valley of the lower Rock River; their main village was on a neck of land where the Rock flowed into the Mississippi. The lands west of the Mississippi had become their principal hunting grounds by then, but they returned to the east bank of the river every summer to plant their fields of corn and squash. After the great

Black Hawk. Oil painting by Charles Bird King, probably done in 1837 on Black Hawk's second visit to Washington, D.C.

cession of 1829 most of the tribal members moved permanently over to the Iowa shore, but one band, led by a 62-year-old warrior named Black Hawk, stood fast. Black Hawk had made annual visits to a British outpost in Canada and still nourished a hope that British military power might revive. He did not participate in the 1829 conference and claimed that the treaty signed by other chieftains had nothing to do with him.

In 1831 Black Hawk finally yielded to government pressure and took his people across to the west bank. He renunciated his land claims and, as he wrote later in his autobiography, "determined to live in peace." However, there was hunger among the Sauk that winter. They had not had a chance to develop new fields, and the government supplies of corn ran short. "Loud lamentations were heard in the camp, by our women and children," he later recalled, and some of the young men crossed the river at night to steal corn from their former fields. Given promises of assistance from Winnebago and Potawatomi leaders, Black Hawk yielded to the cries of his own

The Battle of Bad Axe, as envisioned by an unknown artist.

people, and in April 1832 he led a band of a thousand warriors, together with an assortment of elderly men, women and children, across the Mississippi. He hoped to drive out the usurpers, reoccupy his old village, and replant his traditional cornfields. It was a visionary plan, one almost certain to fail, but it was hardly a declaration of war.

He probably would not have made the crossing had he known of the approach of a large military force sent into the upper Mississippi from St. Louis that spring to overawe and pacify the restless Wisconsin tribes. The commander was General Henry Atkinson, who had wreaked vengeance against the Winnebago five years earlier. Atkinson reached Fort Armstrong, newly erected on an island at the mouth of the Rock River, on April 11, barely a week after Black Hawk made his crossing. Learning of Black Hawk's movement, Atkinson alerted Illinois authorities, who promptly summoned the state militia.

Black Hawk must have learned of Atkinson's approach almost immediately for he made no effort to till the soil. Instead, he led his band up the Rock River to the Winnebago village of the Prophet, his friend and erstwhile ally. Finding that the Prophet did not speak for all of his tribe with his promises of aid, Black Hawk moved farther up the river to a Potawatomi village near the unmarked Wisconsin border. The promises of their leaders also proved empty, and their food bins were even emptier. With his followers hungry and exhausted, Black Hawk was ready to give up. He later wrote: "I concluded to tell my people, that if the White Beaver [General Atkinson] came after us, we would go back—as it was useless to think of stopping or going on without provisions."

On May 14 he sent a delegation under a white flag to the camp of some Illinois militia commanded by Major Isaiah Stillman. Far from accepting the surrender, the undisciplined militia fired at the truce party, killing several Indians. Black Hawk's warriors arrived on the scene and discharged their weapons, watching in astonishment as the Illinois farmers fled in terror. The "battle" was ever after known as Stillman's Run.

Finding no one willing to accept his surrender, Black Hawk

sought to escape to the north and west. He followed the Rock River and its tributary, the Yahara, to the Four Lakes region (now Madison), skirting the south shore of the Fourth Lake (today's Lake Mendota) across the glacial moraine that would later become the campus of the University of Wisconsin. General Atkinson had been forced to stop at Lake Koshkonong to await provisions, and Henry Dodge, commander of the Wisconsin militia, took up the chase. He caught up with the fleeing Indians at the heights overlooking the Wisconsin River opposite present-day Sauk City. After a brief but sharp skirmish, the Indians escaped across the river and made their way overland to the Mississippi. Reaching the Mississippi on August 1, the exhausted and starving Indians hastily built rafts. Only a few made it across the river before the steamboat *Warrior*, dispatched from Fort Crawford, appeared. Ignoring the Indians' white flag, the steamboat opened fire, slaughtering men, women and children indiscriminately. Black Hawk and about 50 of his men fled north along the riverbank. The rest of his followers were slaughtered the following morning by Atkinson's army in what has become known as the Battle of Bad Axe Creek. While the stronger of his remaining men swam to safety across the river, Black Hawk himself surrendered to a party of Winnebagoes. He was turned over to the army, which sent him to Jefferson Barracks in St. Louis under the guard of Lieutenant Jefferson Davis. (Abraham Lincoln also participated in the war as a member of the Illinois militia.) Black Hawk lived to write his memoirs, an eloquent defense of his efforts to maintain a way of life for his dispossessed people.

Ignoring the fact that the Wisconsin tribes had refused to join Black Hawk and some had even aided the army, the government exacted its retribution indiscriminately, and it took it in the form of land. In 1832-33 the Winnebago, Potawatomi and Menominee were forced to sell all their lands south and east of the Wisconsin River, and many of their people were removed west of the Mississippi. In subsequent treaties of 1837 and 1842 the Sioux and the Chippewa surrendered their claims to the remaining lands south of Lake Superior and east of the Mississippi. The Sioux joined their brethren in the Dakotas; the Chippewa retained certain "reserves" in Wisconsin where their descendents reside today. By 1842 the Indian title to all of present-day Wisconsin had been cleared. Immediately upon the initial cessions in 1832-33, the government opened a land office in Green Bay and began dispensing lands at auction, with a minimum price of $1.25 an acre.

▼

Mining the Southwest

It was not the rich prairie soils of the southeast that attracted the first settlers, but the rugged uplands of the southwest. They came as miners rather than farmers, and they arrived long before the Indian title was extinguished. Throughout the region, from the mouth of the Rock River to the mouth of the Wisconsin, veins of lead could be found in limestone crevices at or near the surface of the land. The Indians had begun mining it at least by the middle of the 18th century. They either sold lead to the Spanish in St. Louis or made it into shot themselves once they acquired firearms. Jonathan Carver reported seeing large quantities of lead in a Sauk village on the Wisconsin River in 1766, noting that it came from somewhere in the vicinity of the Blue Mound. The Sauk, other travelers noted, had their women do the digging.

In 1788 Julien Dubuque, a French trader, obtained from the Indians a permit to dig lead on the west side of the Mississippi in a district that included the present-day city of Dubuque. He employed Indians to work the mines and smelted the lead in crude limestone furnaces with wood fires. He shipped the product to St. Louis and continued his trade uninterrupted until the United States acquired the city (including Dubuque's diggings) by the Louisiana Purchase of 1803.

Following the Purchase, the United States government took possession of the rich Missouri mines, and it began a system of leasing mining districts to prospectors. In 1822 the government extended the leasing system to the upper Mississippi and began what can only be called a "lead rush." By 1825 69 permits had been issued, and by 1829 there were 4,253 miners and 52 licensed smelting works in the region. That year more than 13 million pounds of refined lead were sent downriver to St. Louis or east to Lake Michigan. Although the Indians still owned the land, their rights were ignored. The miners simply "squatted" on the land and exploited its mineral wealth. The government endorsed this practice by refusing to enforce the Indians' claims. The early miners lived in their pits, particularly in winter weather, and, likened to a tenacious, burrowing animal that resided in the vicinity, they became known as "badgers."

Among the flotsam of migrants was a Baptist preacher who settled in 1827 on the high ridge that separated waterways flowing north into the Wisconsin River from those flowing southwest into the Mississippi. The site he selected was an ever-flowing watercourse, which gained the name, derived from the preacher's hymns, Jerusalem Spring. Later that year Henry Dodge, who had gained experience in the Missouri mines, came north with his wife, nine children and assorted slaves and built a cabin a few miles away. The following summer prospectors struck lead ore in outcroppings a short distance to the east of the Jerusalem Spring. They found chunks of lead that, when broken open, revealed cubes of silvery mineral known as galena, the purest form of lead ore. News of the strike spread quickly, and before long there were log huts at Jerusalem Spring and along a pathway a half mile away that would soon become known as Shake Rag Street—the name derived from the practice of women who would shake a cloth to signal their miner husbands to come home for the noontime dinner. More deposits were found on the hill adjacent to the two settlements, and because two branches of the Pecatonica River curled around the hill and came together below the mining settlement, the community became known as Mineral Point.

By 1830 the settlement boasted 500 inhabitants, a third of the population of the entire lead region, which itself contained half of all the white population of what is now Wisconsin. It was by then the seat of a new county laid off in the southwestern extremity of the Michigan Territory, named Iowa County. Four years later, when the Indian title was extinguished in the lead region, the government set up a land office, and town lots went up for sale. In the mid-

1830s miners from Cornwall began to arrive in significant numbers. The lead mines of this county in far southwestern England had been worked since Roman times, and when the pits gave out the miners came to America to ply their occupation. Landing at New York or New Orleans, they came by boat up the Mississippi to Galena, Illinois, and by wagon 35 miles overland to Mineral Point.

The same huge land schooners, drawn by teams of oxen, that brought the Cornish in carried the lead out. Some of the finished lead went overland to the newly founded lake ports, Milwaukee and Racine, but most of it went downriver to New Orleans. From there it was shipped to the East Coast where it was made into shot, pipes, sheeting and paint. By 1840 the United States produced annually some 31 million pounds of lead, more than half of which was credited to the Wisconsin Territory.

▼

James Duane Doty, Town Builder

The opening of public land offices at Green Bay and Mineral Point in 1834 triggered a buying frenzy in Wisconsin lands. First in line, quite often, were pioneers from New York, Ohio and Indiana who had squatted on Indian lands awaiting the government's purchase and survey. Having cleared their lands, erected fences, and built log houses, these squatters did not want to have to buy their lands at public auction, for the improvements made the lands more attractive to other bidders. Congress accommodated these people with a land act of 1836 that allowed them to "preempt" the auction by purchasing their farms at the minimum price of $1.25 an acre.

Joining the elbowing and pushing squatters in the land office lines were speculators who sought to buy up large tracts of land at the minimum price and hold them for future sale. The government demanded cash for the public lands; thus the speculators functioned as middlemen, who could offer credit to penniless farmers. Few of these middlemen got rich, however, for land was so abundant that prices rose only very slowly. The speculators who did make money were those who could spot likely sites for towns and cities. And no one was more successful at this game than James Duane Doty.

Although he grew up in western New York, Doty could trace his ancestry to the Pilgrims of the Mayflower. After studying law, he traveled west to Detroit in search of opportunity. Blessed with an extraordinary talent for self-promotion, he became a partner of the most prominent attorney in the settlement. In 1823 President James Monroe named the 24-year-old Doty a federal judge for the district of western Michigan, making him, in effect, the law west of the lake. By canoe he traversed his jurisdiction from Mackinac to Green Bay to Prairie du Chien, eventually settling on the Fox River a few miles from Green Bay. He remained a judge for nine years, during which he came to know intimately the Wisconsin landscape, and with an eye to future profit he made note of every site with commercial possibilities.

James Duane Doty.

Access to transportation not only dictated the location of townsites, it was fundamental to the development of the entire territory. The Fox-Wisconsin canoe route had sufficed the fur traders, but it would not accommodate the transport of grain, flour, lumber or lead. Canals were a possibility, especially after the successful opening of New York's Erie Canal in 1825. Doty toyed with the idea (he promoted, for instance, a canal linking Lake Winnebago with the Rock River), but he ultimately decided that the amount of capital required exceeded the benefit. Roads were the cheapest avenues of communication to construct, and, until the railroads came along, the most efficient to use. As early as 1826 Doty was urging the government to build a road connecting Green Bay with Chicago.

In the summer of 1829 Doty set out on horseback to find a land route between Green Bay and Prairie du Chien. With two circuit-riding attorneys as guides, Doty followed the high ground of the limestone escarpment on the east side of Lake Winnebago. The party curled around the south end of the lake (where Doty would lay out the village of Fond du Lac in 1836) and passed between the First and Second lakes (now Kegonsa and Waubesa) of the Four Lakes district. Passing Blue Mound, the trio followed the ridge that separated the Wisconsin River Valley from the rivers that flowed to the south (the "Military Ridge" or U.S. Highway 18 today). Crossing the Wisconsin near its mouth, the party ended its journey at Fort Crawford.

Doty's report of his journey dramatized the feasibility of the route and aroused the interest of the Army, which saw advantages in a road connecting its Wisconsin forts. In July 1832, at the height of the scare caused by Black Hawk, Congress appropriated $5,000 to lay out a road across Wisconsin, connecting the three forts, Howard, Winnebago and Crawford. Doty, named a civilian member of the survey commission, promptly laid out a route—blazed trees in the forest and crossed sticks on the prairie—that generally followed the path he had taken in 1829. Army engineers built the road between 1835 and 1837. Congress specified that the road be "cut out thirty feet wide; all trees less than twelve inches in diame-

Hauling lead from Mineral Point to Cassville on the Mississippi in the 1830s. An imaginary drawing by I.E. Blair, created for the Wisconsin Highway Commission in 1948.

ter will be felled within six inches of the ground; and those of a greater diameter within twelve inches; the stumps to be hollowed to the center, so as to retain the rain that they may more readily decay." Though built to specifications, the road for many years was little more than a trail of stumps through the wilderness, with crude log bridges across the streams. After completing the main route in 1837, the Army built a spur through Mineral Point to Galena.

With the promise of transportation that would afford access to national and world markets, Doty turned his energies to the founding of townsites. The establishment of Fond du Lac exemplifies his methods. The reedy marshes where the Fond du Lac River lazily rolls into Lake Winnebago had long been a favorite wintering place of French fur traders who found there abundant fish and game. The site lay astride the Military Road, and it had water access to Lake Michigan by way of the Fox River. In 1835 Doty and a Green Bay speculator purchased 3,500 acres in the fertile valley, all of it within the limits of the present-day city of Fond du Lac. With other investors they founded the Fond du Lac Company, which platted the village and erected a double-sized log house that served as a tavern. In 1838 Doty built some frame houses in the town and found farmers to occupy them. He avoided tying up his money in land, preferring instead to invest in the village improvements. Roads, canals and, in the 1850s, railroads attracted him the most. He would then use the profits from these projects to establish another strategically located townsite. He was not averse, however, to investing in towns founded by others when he saw their growth potential. Milwaukee was one of these.

▼

Birth of Milwaukee

Except for Green Bay, the western shore of Lake Michigan had no natural harbors capable of handling commercial shipping. Small rivers, which promised access to the interior, did give rise to some aspiring lake ports, however. The most successful of these by far was Milwaukee. The name was of Indian origin, first recorded as Melleoiki by a French missionary in 1679. The Milwaukee River, which drains a rich landscape to the south and east of Lake Winnebago, meanders into Lake Michigan through substantial bluffs that attracted Indian inhabitants from the earliest times. French traders visited the mouth of the river annually during the 18th century, and beginning in the 1790s there was a tiny community of year-round French and Indian residents.

The story of the "polyglot village that became a metropolis" began in 1818 when Solomon Juneau, an agent of Astor's American Fur Company, set up a trading post on the bank of the river. Juneau was an enterprising man, but this was not immediately evident because the Indians owned the land and were his only customers. A map of the Michigan Territory published in 1830 pictured an Indian village with two white families, Juneau and his brother, on the "Milwauky River." The Indian cessions of 1833 opened the way for the development but did not immediately remove Indians from the scene. A caravan of ox teams carried many of them westward (probably to Iowa or Nebraska) in 1838, but blanketed Indians could be seen patrolling the streets of the lakeside village as late as the 1850s.

On the heels of the Indian cession in the fall of 1833 Juneau formed a partnership with Green Bay speculator Morgan Martin (who had accompanied Doty on his 1829 overland journey), by which Juneau gave Martin a half-interest in his preemptive claim to the lands along the east side of the river in return for Martin's money and expertise. The following spring the pair enclosed "the best parts" of Juneau's claim with posts, logs and a "handsome little building," all designed to substantiate Juneau's claim when the land was surveyed and put up for sale at the Green Bay land office. Before the lands went up for sale, Byron Kilbourn, public surveyor for the Michigan Territory, posted a claim to the lands on the west side of the Milwaukee River. He rejected a Martin-Juneau offer to cooperate, and as a result the city originated as two townsites, Juneautown and Kilbourntown.

By July 1835, when the Green Bay office began to offer Milwaukee lands for sale, squatters had taken possession of the site "in swarms," and Juneau was getting $500 to $600 bids for half-acre lots within his claim before he even acquired them from the government. When the land office finally opened, Juneau/Martin and Kilbourn gained possession of their claims at little more than the government minimum of $1.25 an acre.

In the ferocious land speculation that enveloped Wisconsin in 1835-36 Milwaukee was the biggest prize of all because of its potential as a lake port. By early 1836 Juneau was a rich man, reputedly worth $100,000 and doing a daily business of $8,000 to $10,000. Judge Doty was in the midst of the land fever. At the opening of the public sale he purchased $5,000 in tracts at the mouth of the Milwaukee River and sold them a year later at a 500 percent profit. Kilbourn, on the other hand, lost much of his fortune in an ill-fated effort to dig a canal connecting his portion of Milwaukee with the Rock River.

A traveler who arrived in Milwaukee in July 1836 reported a village of 50 houses and 1,208 people where, he wrote in astonishment, "18 months ago there were but two families!" The disparity between population and available shelter was explained, in part, by other accounts. One journalist noted that "Everyday, almost, new frames were erected. Men's hats were crammed with maps of paper towns." Owners of vacant lots commanded high rents for the privilege of selling goods on their property. One observer claimed that profits could be made simply by "standing around, i.e., watching the land market for bargains."

A speculative mania engrossed the entire country in 1836 as Americans of every social order sought instant wealth through investments in city lots, wharves, canals and railroads. President Andrew Jackson, a frontiersman accustomed to calculating wealth in terms of soil that could be sifted or coin that could be bit into, blamed the speculative fever on the proliferation of banks and paper money. In early 1836 he directed the treasury to accept only gold or silver coin in payment for public lands. The Specie Circular, which went into effect on August 15, brought the frenzied trading in Wisconsin to an abrupt halt. Gold and silver had always been in short supply in the West; people traded by barter or in paper notes issued by local banks. The optimism that had sparked the boom collapsed, as investors who had worked on borrowed money found themselves unable to repay their loans, meet interest demands, or pay their tax assessments. Government foreclosure and the sale of lands for taxes became a symbol of the hard times.

Milwaukee's journalists—the village boasted four newspapers by 1837—professed to see a silver lining in the cloud of depression. Admitting that town building in advance of the development of the rural hinterland had been a mistake, they claimed that the hard times in the eastern United States would "send crowds of the very bone and sinew of society to our harbor, seeking employment and bringing into speedy cultivation the…healthful regions in the interior." Nevertheless, a shortage of money, one symptom of the nationwide depression, lasted into the 1840s. Not until 1842 did the Milwaukee press report a revival in the real estate market, streets busy with wagons of produce from the interior, and an influx of immigrants.

One consequence of the national depression was that federal support for internal improvements dried up. The water at the mouth of the Milwaukee River was too shallow for deep-draft boats, and cargoes had to be transferred to barges to reach the port. Calls for federal funds to dredge a harbor fell on deaf ears, even when the citizens, reminding the government of the sums they had paid into its coffers in return for land, claimed harbor improvement "as a matter of right, justly our due." One hothead, mindful of the growing rift between North and South in the country, threatened that if Congress failed to make an appropriation, Wisconsin people would "take the matter into their own hands ... excite the slaves in the South to insurrection ... secede from the Union ... establish an Indian government on Doty's purchase, and make Doty our chief."

Despite the depression, the village grew steadily, adding new businesses every year. Although the first inhabitants were mostly men, enough women resided in the town by 1837 to warrant the opening of a millinery and dressmaking shop. The proprietor, Miss S.E. Chamberlin, announced the availability of silk and cotton hose, whale-bone foundations, "fancy Grecian-colored straws" and assorted belt ribbons. She also promised that hats "in the most fashionable style" could be put together on short notice. By 1842, 25 retail stores were in operation, and the revival of trade induced one journalist to effuse "the stores of our merchants are well supplied with as fine assortments of goods as can be found in the west, and our streets are thronged day after day with teams from the interior, bringing to market the produce of the country."

While the federal government dawdled on harbor improvement, entrepreneurs filled the void by constructing piers far enough into the lake to accommodate deep-draft lake vessels. The first, completed in 1843, brought a handsome profit to its owner through dockage fees, and it sparked a flurry of warehouse construction in its vicinity. The lake trade was the basis of Milwaukee's future growth because the city and its hinterland depended largely on the exchange of products with the settled East. The importance of transportation costs was reflected in the fact that wheat, which sold for 62 cents a bushel in Milwaukee, commanded 87 cents in Buffalo. Wheat, flour and lead were the city's principal exports. Furs, by the mid-1840s, were negligible, of less importance than the export of cowhides and sheepskins.

Milwaukee had a population of 3,000 in 1843, nearly all migrants from New England and New York. In that year, however, Germans began arriving in substantial numbers, followed by Irish (most of whom had stopped initially in Boston or New York) and other Europeans. By 1850 the city numbered more than 20,000. A traveler from Ohio who had come to Wisconsin looking for farmland described Milwaukee in 1847 as the busiest place he had ever seen.

A fellow has to go a side at a time and then can hardly get along the sidewalk. A man not used to the like of such things to come here and see the number of wheat teams could hardly believe himself. Every kind of mechanism is a going on in this place from street hawking to manufacturing steam engines and every kind of citizens from the rude Norwegian to the polished Italian. This is a great place for professional men such as Legal, Physical, Dental, Dogmatical and all the other als. But it certenly is the d__mdst place for Old Maids that it ever has been my lot to see before. They go in such droves along the side walks that it kept me a dogeing all the time to keep clear of dresses or being struck by a bustle when they are a swinging them along.

Predicted another enthusiastic visitor: "Milwaukie ... is destined to be the chief commercial and manufacturing city of this WESTERN EMPIRE." During these same years, 1836 to 1848, while Milwaukee was growing from speculator's dream to bustling seaport, Wisconsin evolved from lightly governed wilderness to statehood in the American union. Commercial and political development went hand in hand.

▼

Wisconsin Becomes a Territory

In 1836 Michigan entered the Union as a state, carefully paired with Arkansas so as to maintain the balance between free and slave states in the United States Senate. A bill creating a separate Wisconsin Territory swished through Congress at the same time. The only controversy involved boundaries. Ohio disputed Michigan's boundary in the south, claiming the lands around the western end of Lake Erie. North of Lake Michigan, Wisconsin claimed what is now the Upper Peninsula. Congress yielded to Ohio's demands in the south and compensated Michigan by giving it more of the Upper Peninsula than Michigan residents had ever dreamed of attaining. Congress drew the dividing line between Michigan and Wisconsin along two rivers whose headwaters were not far apart, the Menominee flowing into Green Bay and the Montreal, which flowed into Lake Superior. To the west, the Wisconsin Territory extended as far as the Missouri River, thus embracing present-day Iowa, Minnesota and the eastern half of the Dakotas. A census taken in 1836 revealed 22,218 white inhabitants, almost half of whom lived west of the Mississippi in Dubuque and Des Moines counties.

Although the governor was to be appointed by the president, the territorial Organic Act authorized a popularly elected two-house legislature, which was to meet annually. Ten days after Congress approved the territorial bill President Andrew Jackson appointed Colonel Henry Dodge governor of the new territory. A hero of the Black Hawk War, Dodge was immensely popular in the lead region, by far the best populated part of the territory. Dodge, like many of the miners, had moved to Wisconsin from Missouri, and he had strong connections among Missouri politicians in Washington. Because of the Missouri element, the lead region had a strong southern flavor, and it was solidly Democratic in national politics. Dodge was a natural choice for governor.

▼

Selecting a Capital

Judge Doty was as well known in the Wisconsin Territory as Dodge, but his salty business dealings had made him enemies. The president removed him as a judge in 1832, and he lost a bid to become territorial delegate to Congress in 1835. Doty thereafter turned his full energies to land speculation. On the day that Dodge was sworn in as governor, July 4, 1836, Doty was laying out the streets for a new village in the area of the Four Lakes.

The incomparable beauty of the Four Lakes region had long attracted Doty, as well as other speculators. Because of its central location, it was a prime site for a capital city, and it held promise of good communications with all parts of the territory. The Military Road ran along the north shore of the Fourth Lake, later named Mendota, and a projected railroad connecting Milwaukee with the Mississippi River was certain to pass through the area. Doty even had plans to build a canal connecting Lake Mendota with the Wisconsin River, a mere 20 miles to the northwest.

When the Four Lakes region went up for sale at the Green Bay land office in 1835, speculators quickly snapped up most of the lakeshore tracts. Even so, in the spring of 1836 the narrow isthmus between the Third and Fourth lakes was still government-owned. In April of that year Doty, in partnership with a half-breed who resided on Lake Mendota (its only resident), purchased the tract, amounting to about 1,360 acres. On June 1 Doty and other investors formed the Four Lakes Company, and Doty was made "trustee" with power to plat a city and sell the lots. On the future metropolis Doty bestowed the name "City of Madison" in honor of the ex-president who had died earlier that summer. In early July Doty wandered among the hazel bushes and stunted oaks blackened by prairie fires, laying out future streets on a grid pattern. On the high ground between the two lakes he laid out a square "to be used for county or territorial purposes." "Wiskonsan Avenue" ran from lake to lake, interrupted by the square. At right angles to this street, he projected broad "Washington Avenue," with a "Railroad from the Mississippi to Milwaukee" running right up the avenue to the capitol square. Remarking to his partner that Madison would some day become the territorial capital, Doty set off for the temporary capital at Belmont with a scheme for turning his vision into reality.

A week after his inauguration Governor Dodge designated Belmont as the temporary capital of the territory and ordered the newly elected Legislature to meet there in October. The governor almost immediately had occasion to regret his choice, for the townsite, which had been platted as recently as May 15, was utterly unprepared to host a government. It lay 12 miles southwest of Mineral Point in the heart of the lead region, astride the wagon road to Galena. One visitor grumbled that it was "without wood, water, in an open bleak prairie, with no communication" to other parts of the territory. Speculators immediately flocked to the place and began buying up town lots. By the time the Legislature assembled at the end of October the village consisted of three taverns, three lodging houses, a printing office, an unfinished stable and a two-story building with a store front that served as the capitol.

Governor Dodge may have chosen this quiet location in order to avoid jousting among the more established communities, but he reopened the regional competition by announcing that the first business of the Legislature would be to select a permanent capital. Advocates for Green Bay, Milwaukee and Mineral Point immediately stepped forth. A bloc of Des Moines legislators, meanwhile, demanded a site west of the Mississippi, either at Dubuque or Burlington. Into this political cauldron rode Judge Doty on the second of November.

The bill for the establishment of a capital initially named Dubuque as the temporary site and Fond du Lac (founded by Doty earlier that year) as the permanent location. After a day's debate a Des Moines delegate successfully moved to substitute Madison as the permanent location. (He later appeared on the books as a Madison landowner.) Amidst heated debate over three days, 16 substitute sites were moved and voted down. When approved at last, the bill located the capital at Burlington while buildings were constructed at Madison for the permanent seat. How the Legislature finally agreed upon Madison remains an enduring mystery. The centrality of its location was certainly a factor, but those who recalled the battle in later years were inclined to credit the machinations of Judge Doty. "While others were planning," a Green Bay delegate noted, "Judge Doty was acting." The nature of Doty's activities was revealed in the reminiscence of another contemporary:

> *Doty supplied himself with a full stock of buffalo robes, and went around camping with the members, and making them comfortable as he could, until he organized a sufficient vote in the Legislature to make Madison the permanent capital. ... The winter was a cold, dreary one, and Doty with his buffalo robes had been a real blessing to the members, and he also accommodated them with town lots in the new, wild, uninhabited town of Madison.*

Doty's buffalo robes, apparently acquired from a Sioux village on the Mississippi, are a fixture in Wisconsin lore, but his distribution of city lots (16 of which went directly to members of the Legislature) may have been more influential. Equally important was Doty's establishment of a broad base of ownership in Madison that would ward off future efforts to change the location of the capital. By the spring of 1837 he had sold, or given, portions of Madison to wealthy speculators and prominent officials, including the territorial delegate to Congress, the chief justice and the governor's son, Augustus C. Dodge.

The Legislature placed Doty on the three-man commission charged with supervising the construction of public buildings, for which Congress had appropriated $20,000. The site for the capitol was cleared in the spring of 1838, and construction was begun immediately so the Legislature could meet there that fall, a year ahead of schedule. Congress made the move from Burlington more urgent when it detached Iowa from Wisconsin that summer and erected the Iowa Territory. The specifications called for a stone building 30 feet high with columned piazzas in the front and rear. Surmounting the building was a dome 26 feet in diameter covered with tin. When the legislators gathered in the new capital city in November, they found a few log cabins and two hotels. The capitol was not yet ready, but the governor, Legislature and Supreme Court were able to move in within a few days. Doty, who had managed the entire affair, was the most popular man in the territory. That fall he was elected to Congress as territorial delegate. He was at the height of his political career. He was also on the edge of a precipice.

Doty's descent into disfavor and poverty began with the first session of the Legislature in Madison in the winter of 1838-39. The new capitol had been constructed of green oak, and the floor boards shrank when the single fireplace and stove were lighted. Custodians covered the floor with straw to keep out the draft, but still the ink froze in the wells of the legislators' desks. The depression, which had begun with Jackson's Specie Circular and the financial panic of 1837, further darkened the legislators' mood. Egged on by delegates from the lead region, where Doty had never been popular, the Legislature began an investigation of Doty's expenditure of funds on the capitol building and a separate inquiry into the validity of the title to the land on which the building stood.

King Street in Madison, 1851, with the new capitol in the background. Drawn by traveler-artist Johann B. Wengler.

After the Legislature departed for home, the investigation was taken up by Moses M. Strong, the United States attorney for the territory. A resident of Mineral Point, Strong was the new political power in the lead region, and he began what can only be described as a crusade to destroy Doty. A 10-year legal battle ensued in which both men lost. It impoverished Doty and threw a permanent shadow over his political career.

As territorial delegate, Doty aligned himself with the anti-Jackson men in Congress, who some years earlier had adopted the label "Whigs." He reaped his reward when the Whigs won the presidency in the "log cabin and hard cider" campaign of 1840. Named governor of Wisconsin, he took up residence in Madison in 1841, inaugurating three years of political turmoil. The lead region was solidly Democratic, and it had powerful voices in Henry Dodge and Moses Strong. Doty could count on some support among the Yankees of Milwaukee and Racine, but the Whigs never developed a state organization. Doty and the Legislature grappled in daily battles over every item on the political agenda—Indian treaties, village post offices, erection of counties, chartering of banks and improvements in transportation. In the shadows lingered the financially draining lawsuits pushed by Moses Strong. Most embarrassing of all to Doty was the election of Dodge as delegate to Congress. Dodge aligned himself with the Democrats and barraged the Whig President, John Tyler, with a stream of complaints about Doty's management of Wisconsin. When Doty's term ended in 1844, Tyler, who was himself at odds with his own party, replaced him. The new governor was a colorless congressman from New York who had no chance to make his mark on the territory. The Democrats returned to the White House in 1844 with the election of James K. Polk, and Dodge took over the governor's chair in Madison.

▼

Statehood

The legislature that assembled in Madison in 1846 was markedly different from the first assembly that had met at Belmont a decade earlier. New counties that had not been in existence in 1836 now sent members—Walworth, Waukesha, Rock and Racine, all in the southeastern part of the territory. The southeast had outdistanced the lead region, and its population was predominantly transplanted Yankee, with an increasing assortment of Germans and Irish. As in 1836, not one member of the Legislature was a native of Wisconsin, and it was still predominantly Democratic in political allegiance. The building in which it met had also changed. The entrance was embellished with an eight-column piazza and a balustrade. The basement, long the domicile of the village's hogs, was deepened for the storage of firewood and later for offices. Workers had mowed the hazel brush and grubbed the oak stumps, replacing them with maples and elms.

Through the early 1840s Governor Doty had lobbied for statehood, but his had been a lonely voice. So long as Congress paid the territory's debts and financed its road and harbor improvements, the citizenry had little use for the responsibilities of state sovereignty. The Democrats' return to national power in 1845 changed all that, however. President Polk, reviving the Jacksonian tradition of limited federal involvement in the economy, vetoed bills for inter-

A prairie oak opening south of Madison, 1832. Pencil drawing by Adolph Hoeffler.

nal improvements, and the money for Wisconsin's roads and harbors dried up. Statehood, which entailed a bonus from Congress of 500,000 acres in federal lands, as well as a section in each township for the maintenance of schools, suddenly seemed more inviting. Congress was more receptive as well. The outbreak of the Mexican War in 1846 exacerbated sectional tensions, and Northerners were eager to add another free state to balance the recent admissions of Florida and Texas.

In the spring of 1846 the Legislature authorized a popular referendum on statehood, which was overwhelmingly approved. That summer Congress obligingly passed an Enabling Act, which permitted Wisconsin to hold a convention and draft a state constitution. The act set the western boundary at a line drawn due south from the western end of Lake Superior to the St. Croix River and thence along the St. Croix and Mississippi rivers, the present boundary with Minnesota.

The convention that met in the fall of 1846 to draft a constitution for the new state was heavily Democratic, and it reflected that party's Jacksonian biases. A draft submitted by Moses Strong prohibited banks and extended the suffrage to white males only. However, it did allow immigrants who had applied for citizenship to vote, and it granted married women a right to own property independently of their husbands, a reform that was far in advance of most other states. These provisions excited spirited debate, but all were retained, although the question of Negro suffrage was submitted to the voters separately. Each region of the territory reacted differently to these liberal/democratic issues, but enough opposition surfaced to defeat the constitution, 14,000 in favor to 20,000 against. Negro suffrage went down to defeat by a similar margin.

A second convention in 1848 was more discreet. Its constitution omitted any mention of women or blacks, and it left the question of voting rights to the Legislature, subject to public approval. The Legislature was also allowed to charter banks, subject to popular referendum, but it was prohibited from incurring debts for the construction of roads or canals. On the other hand, the constitution did embrace the concept of state-supported public education, a reform that had only recently been introduced among the states of the Northeast. Voters approved the new document by an overwhelming majority. The principal opposition came from an antislavery party, born of the Mexican War, which objected to the "white male" restriction on voting.

1848, the year in which Wisconsin entered the Union, was a momentous one in world history. It was a year of revolutions in Europe that sent a stream of political refugees to the United States and to Wisconsin. It was the year in which Karl Marx published the Communist Manifesto, inaugurating a century and a half of ideological warfare between capitalism and communism. The treaty signed that year that ended the War with Mexico brought into the American orbit the Southwest from Texas to California, and completed the republic's march to the Pacific. The discovery of gold in California triggered a rush of "forty-niners" that populated California and breathed new life into the sectional struggle between North and South. The pace of events in 1848 was truly dizzying, and the new state would soon be swept into the maelstrom.

▼

Travelers' Guide
Early Settlement

Blackhawk Ridge Recreation Area, Highway 78 northwest of Madison. Historic site on the hilltop from which Chief Black Hawk directed the 1832 battle.

City of Prairie du Chien, Highway 35/18; (608) 326-8555. Site of an important Indian settlement and outpost for the American Fur Trading Co. Historic markers identify the town's old homes and other historic buildings.

Doty Cabin, 701 Lincoln St., Neenah; (414) 751-4744. Reconstruction of the home of James Duane Doty, Wisconsin's second territorial governor.

First Capitol State Park, County G north of Belmont; (608) 987-2122. Site of the 1836 capital of the Wisconsin Territory, with the original Council House and Supreme Court buildings.

Fort Crawford Medical Museum, 717 S. Beaumont St., Prairie du Chien; (608) 326-6960. Displays on the history of medicine housed in the reconstructed 1830s Fort Crawford Hospital.

Heritage Hill State Park, 2640 S. Webster Ave., Green Bay; (800) 721-5150, (414) 448-5150. Fort Howard's original hospital building and officers' quarters depict circa-1836 military life. Events feature French and Indian War and War of 1812 encampments.

Hoard Historical Museum and National Dairy Shrine, 407 Merchants Ave., Fort Atkinson; (414) 563-7769. Includes exhibits documenting the Black Hawk War.

Military Ridge State Trail, Verona to Dodgeville; (608) 935-2315. Ride your bicycle 40 miles on a crushed-limestone railroad bed that follows the path of the old Military Road.

Historic Indian Agency House, Agency House Road, Portage; (608) 742-6362. Home built in 1832 for the U.S. Indian agent to the Winnebago, near the portage between the Fox and Wisconsin rivers.

Surgeons' Quarters, East Highway 33, Portage; (608) 742-2949. The only remaining building of Fort Winnebago, built in 1828.

White Pillars, 403 N. Broadway, De Pere; (414) 336-3877. The first bank building in Wisconsin, built in 1836, and the home of the De Pere Historical Society Museum.

Mining

Badger Mine and Museum, 279 Estey St., Shullsburg; (608) 965-4860. An early lead mine and exhibits of mining tools.

Pendarvis, 114 Shake Rag St., Mineral Point; (608) 987-2122. A collection of restored lead-miners' cottages, and a State Historic Site.

Platteville Mining Museum, 405 E. Main St., Platteville; (608) 348-3301. A restored lead mine with exhibits on area mining.

St. John Mine, Highway 133, Potosi; (608) 763-2121. Hand-dug lead mine used by Indians and immigrant miners.

Chapter 4

WISCONSIN'S CIVIL WAR

A traveler landing at Milwaukee in 1848 would have found newly graded and graveled streets, sidewalks paved with slabs of limestone and stores of cream-colored brick. The population numbered 14,000, about 40 percent of it German. The principal industry in town was flour milling, and wheat was its main export. Farmers brought their produce to the city by wagon, thus limiting the city's hinterland to a radius of 40 or 50 miles. However, railroad construction would soon extend Milwaukee's economic reach across the state. The Milwaukee and Mississippi Railroad reached Madison in 1854 and Prairie du Chien in 1857.

Twenty-five miles south of Milwaukee was Racine, another fast-growing wheat port with a population of about 4,000, making it the second-largest city in the state. Ten miles farther along the lakeshore was Southport (renamed Kenosha in 1850), the third largest at 3,000. The hinterland of these milling centers was rolling country of prairie and oak groves, rapidly being brought under tillage. Nearly all farm houses were frame buildings, the original log cabins having been converted into stables and tool sheds.

The road west from Milwaukee was little more than a pathway through the woods that wound its way over the rugged Kettle Moraine. A traveler who made the trip by stage complained of being "shaken, or rather hurled, unmercifully hither and thither" upon a road that was not a road at all, "but a succession of hills and holes and water-pools, in which first one wheel sank and then the other, while the opposite one stood high up in the air." Watertown, on the Rock River, was a "newly sprung-up, infant town," of about 2,000. As a market community, midway between Milwaukee and Madison, with access to the Mississippi, Watertown was thought to have a boundless future and speculators were furiously trading town lots in 1848.

A few miles beyond Watertown, the trees thinned out and the road entered a level grassland, the Sun Prairie, that extended some 25 miles west to the Four Lakes. Madison was described by a traveler in

Wisconsin cities and villages, 1848.

1848 as "a pretty little town" of about a thousand people. West of Madison traveling conditions improved as the Military Road followed a ridge that divided the waters of the southwestern part of the state. The road ended at Prairie du Chien, a sleepy village that had changed little since the days of the fur trade. Timber speculators were beginning to stake out lands in the Chippewa and St. Croix valleys to the north, however, and before long Prairie du Chien would be graced by the stately mansions of lumber barons.

▼

The Population Surges

The population of Wisconsin was growing at a furious pace. In the six years before statehood it had increased from 45,000 people to nearly 250,000. It would double again in the next six years. Migrants continued to stream into Wisconsin from New England and New York, as they had for the past decade, settling in Racine and Southport and populating the tier of counties along the Illinois border. Janesville, on the Rock River, was an almost purely Yankee community. A German visitor explained the value of this sort of people in a frontier community:

> The talent of a New Englander is universal. He is a good farmer, an excellent schoolmaster, a very respectable preacher, a capital lawyer, a sagacious physician, an able editor, a thriving merchant, a shrewd pedlar and a most industrious tradesman. Being thus able to fill all the important posts of society, only a few emigrants from New England are required to imprint a lasting character on a new state, even if their number should be much inferior to that of the other settlers.

Yankee migration to Wisconsin was a steady flow; the spurt in population growth that began in the late 1840s was due to massive migration from Europe. The transatlantic movement of peoples has often been described as a product of "push" and "pull"—the repellant force of Old World conditions combined with the lure of land and opportunity in the New. Immigrants themselves were the best advertisement for America, as they wrote home to friends and relatives with tales of New World bounty and the opportunities for success. The key "push" factor was social and economic change in Europe that created a population surplus. Improvements in agriculture in Germany and the British Isles reduced the need for farm laborers and induced landlords to evict tenants and cottagers. The rise of manufacturing centers absorbed some of the surplus population, but the principal safety valve was the New World. In some parts of Germany half of the children were born out of wedlock because young people were not allowed to marry until they found a place to live—or agreed to move to America.

In the mid-1840s a natural disaster quickened the flow of people. From Scandinavia to Ireland the potato had become a dietary staple for the poor. (Ironically, the introduction of the potato was largely responsible for the spurt of population growth that began in the 18th century, for the potato, when cooked with milk, provides nearly all the daily nutritional requirements for a family.) A blight struck in the mid-1840s that rotted the potatoes in the fields. Famine haunted parts of Norway and Ireland and the survivors fled to America. Germany escaped the famine with good harvests of grain, but that country suffered from political turmoil. A republican revolution against the Prussian and Austrian monarchies in 1848 was suppressed by imperial troops and many of the "radicals" fled to America. Carl Schurz, pausing in England on his way to Milwaukee, declared: "If I cannot be the citizen of a free Germany, then I would at least be a citizen of free America."

The routes were many. Irish and Germans commonly landed in New York and traveled westward by way of the Erie Canal and the Great Lakes. Scandinavians usually landed at Quebec and filtered inland by various paths. Typical, perhaps, was the journey of Ole Osterud in 1854 from Hurdalen, Norway, to a Norwegian settlement at Muskego, Racine County. Although he had only three days of formal schooling, he had been taught to read and write by his uncle, a schoolmaster. After his arrival in Wisconsin, where he was welcomed at the farm of Tosten Sogaarden, he wrote a lengthy description of his trip to his brother in Norway.

Osterud's party sailed from Christiana on the 10th of April and spent five days beating around the southwest coast of Norway. From Bergen the vessel struck westward into the Atlantic, passing the Shetland Islands two days later. The ship sailed to the north of the islands, using them as shelter against a southeastern gale. Midway across the Atlantic a severe storm blasted away part of the ship's railing but failed to frighten the passengers—or so Osterud claimed. On May 6 the captain sounded the outermost of the Grand Banks and paused to fish. They dropped unbaited hooks to the bottom and the cod, lying in thick schools, were hooked in the belly, tail or back. The party caught 70 in three days and resumed the voyage. For a week or more the boat drifted outside the Gulf of St. Lawrence along with 36 other vessels, held up by fog and icebergs. They sailed up the gulf for several days before sighting land on the 25th. The ship landed at Quebec on June 1, six weeks after it left Norway.

The ship captain arranged the party's transportation to Milwaukee. The charge was $10, plus 75 cents for each pound of baggage in excess of 100 pounds. A huge steamboat, carrying 800 people, took the party upriver to Montreal. Osterud described the passengers as including "Norwegians, Swedes, Irish and German, black negroes and brown Indians." From Montreal horses and wagons hauled the party up the Ottawa River to the Ottawa-Ontario canal that had been built by the Canadians after the War of 1812. A canal boat carried them to Kingston and a larger vessel ferried them across Lake Ontario to Hamilton. From Hamilton they went by rail to Detroit and another train carried them on to Chicago. Osterud took a steamboat to Milwaukee where he hired a wagoneer to drive him to Muskego. He described for his brother his first reaction to America:

> *We were comfortable while we were on the ocean compared with what we experienced going inland. There was always so much commotion and there were so many transfers. And everything had to go in such a hurry as if life were at stake. If one were not on time, one would have to wait until*

the next day, which we surely learned in Chicago. When we had almost finished loading our baggage, the boat started, leaving several passengers, some of whose baggage was on the boat and some on the pier. They did not arrive in Milwaukee until the following day.

And so we have arrived in good condition. Lars Gullickson bought a farm for nine hundred dollars the first day we were here. I must tell you something about how things are here. The houses are generally not large, but the farms are beautiful.

Tosten's circumstances are exactly as he has written. He has a large farm and much stock. I have not counted his cows, but I have seen that he has seven calves, two large oxen, twenty-three geese and a lot of chickens. As far as food is concerned here in America, there is an abundance. Even though I tell you so, you will perhaps all think it a falsehood. Concerning wages, conditions are as you have heard before. Today I was offered twelve dollars a month and keep, but I did not accept, for I expect to get more.

Lars Gulickson was an unusual immigrant to be able to afford a farm on arriving. Most had to serve as hired hands for some years before they built up the capital to buy land, livestock and seed. Osterud himself probably did not acquire a farm in Muskego, for two years later he moved on to the Red River Valley of Minnesota. Some immigrants never succeeded in acquiring a farm, or perhaps never intended to do so. The Irish seemed, on the whole, to prefer earning a living by pick and shovel and wheelbarrow. Most of the Irish communities in Wisconsin were located near harbor, canal or railroad "improvements." Only about half of the male population of Wisconsin owned land in 1850.

The frontier has long been regarded as the great "leveler" in American history, creating opportunities for the poor and forcing novelty on the rich. The frontier experience did have some effect on Wisconsin society, but not as great as some have supposed. Wisconsin, even in 1850, was not an egalitarian community of small, independent freeholders. Wealth was concentrated in the east, notably in Milwaukee County where eight of the 11 richest men resided. Forty-six Milwaukeans were worth at least $100,000, the equivalent of being a multimillionaire today. The top 10 percent owned 80 percent of the wealth, a ratio not far from that of the United States in the 1990s. Across the state, in Trempealeau County on the Mississippi, the top 10 percent owned only 40 percent of the

Lithograph of Milwaukee in 1854.

wealth. The frontier was thus of some leveling influence, but it did not create a society of equals.

There was a close relationship between wealth and nativity, which suggests that those who brought funds with them were the most likely to succeed in the western environment. American-born men possessed several times as much property as the foreign-born. Men born in New York or New England possessed the most property, on the average. Next came those born in Ohio and other Midwestern states. Lowest in property-holding, on average, were Wisconsin natives, many of whom were descended from fur traders. Among the foreign-born, the wealthiest in 1850 were those from England and Scotland, who in fact ranked ahead of Wisconsin natives. Continental immigrants possessed the least amount of property among the white residents of the state.

▼

Status of Women, Indians and Blacks

In 1848 a newly arrived German immigrant described middle-class Milwaukee women in this fashion:

The women appear stylishly dressed, sometimes on horseback, more commonly seated next to their husbands on the wagon seat. Silk dresses, hats and silk veils, silk parasols and umbrellas, are nothing scarce. This sex receives great attention here and little work is expected therefrom. In this connection it may be well to suggest that a young man who contemplates emigration in order to settle down here, pay his addresses to a girl, for here the choice is meagre. Moreover, German girls are willing to work and do not smoke, whereas some American women do.

The visitor no doubt exaggerated the amount of leisure time that women had, or perhaps he was simply expressing a male viewpoint. Farm wives and women from poor families certainly worked as hard as the men did, but it is nevertheless likely that women were accorded more respect in a frontier society. Men had far outnumbered women in Wisconsin from the beginning of settlement. In 1840 there were eight men for every five women, and in 1850 the ratio was still six to five. A Norwegian immigrant grumbled about "the unusual amount of consideration which is everywhere shown toward women. This tendency often goes to extremes." He attributed it to the fact that women were in "heavy demand" because "marriage means not only happiness but also money" to a pioneer farmer.

For a young woman with funds to travel westward, the frontier did promise opportunity. In 1842 Racheline Wood urged her sister in Vermont to come to Platteville and take a position as head of a proposed girl's school: "You can earn money three times as fast here as there," she predicted, "and I think you will enjoy better health. We have a good society better than any other place in the mining section of the country." Wood's one bit of advice was to secure a good supply of fashionable clothes before leaving because "dresses were in as short supply as dollars" in Platteville.

Teaching was one of several occupations to which women gained access in the Civil War era. Because schools were not graded, toddlers mingled with burly teenagers in a classroom and it was long thought that only men could control the melee. Catherine Beecher thought otherwise and began a crusade to place women in the classroom. The daughter of a prominent New England evangelist and sister of Harriet Beecher Stowe, Catherine Beecher visited Milwaukee in 1850 to inspect a Female Seminary that was run by the wife of a Congregational minister. Beecher donated money to convert the school into a nondenominational college for women, devoted to intellectual advancement and vocational training. In 1852 the school was renamed the Milwaukee Female College and in 1895 it became Milwaukee-Downer College. Many of its graduates became schoolteachers.

In the end, however, it was not Beecher's lectures but economics that wrought the social change that placed women in the classroom. School boards found that women were willing to work for less money than men and women were able to vary their teaching schedules when children were needed for planting or harvest. For commercial reasons, rather than for their supposed set of feminine values, women replaced men in the schoolroom, and elementary education became almost exclusively a feminine activity.

Despite their relatively high status, Wisconsin women suffered nearly as many legal disabilities as those in the eastern United States. If married, they were part of their husband's estate and they had no independent access to the law courts. As already noted, they were severely restricted in job activities. One of the objectives of the early trade unions in the lakeside cities was to keep females from becoming tailors, shoemakers, cigarmakers or printers. Mathilde Franziska Anneke, a political refugee from Germany, established the first women's newspaper in Milwaukee. She not only advocated that women be given the vote, but she wanted to employ them as compositors for her paper. The men at the print shop, themselves German, refused to set type for her. She got the paper printed at another shop, but the venture folded after only six issues.

Although women were not given the vote, they gained some legal rights as a result of the reform movement that swept the North in the decades before the Civil War. In 1850 the Wisconsin Legislature passed a law that enabled them to possess property independent of their husbands'. A law of 1855 allowed wives to dispose of their own wages without their husbands' interference, but only in cases where the husband was unable to provide support. Suffrage and legal equality were reforms of the far distant future. Women nevertheless contributed to the reform movement through voluntary societies that agitated for social change. In 1853 Wisconsin became the first state to abolish capital punishment. The following year a popular referendum approved statewide prohibition of liquor, but when the Legislature passed a statute to that effect, the governor vetoed it.

Wisconsin's Indian population was not enumerated until the census of 1860 and then not very systematically. The census takers found a total of 1,017 "civilized Indians," 404 of them "half breeds." The Indians counted in the census were "Indians taxed," that is, property owners who paid taxes. The census took note of "broken bands and scattered remnants of tribes" who lived in poverty and paid no taxes. Their numbers can only be guessed. In addition, census takers recorded the existence of "tribal" Indians who lived on reservations in the northern part of the state. These tribes—Chippewa, Menominee, Oneida and Stockbridge—were not tallied in the census, but government Indian agents estimated their number at 8,000.

The first blacks in Wisconsin had arrived as slaves, brought to the territory by Missourians who came to work the lead mines. Slavery was prohibited by the Northwest Ordinance, but there was no enforcement mechanism. The census of 1840 counted 185 free blacks and 11 slaves in the territory. By 1850 slavery had disappeared and the number of free blacks had risen to 635. It would nearly double again to 1,171 by 1860. Although blacks were not allowed to serve in the militia, they did enjoy greater legal rights than in other Northern states. Wisconsin had no law against interracial marriage, and in Milwaukee as of 1850 five of the 25 married black men had white wives. Blacks were also allowed to own property, engage in any occupation, send their children to public schools, appeal to the courts, testify against whites, serve on juries, and hold public meetings.

Most blacks lived in Milwaukee and Racine where they dominated the barbering and hairdressing trades. They also worked as sailors, artisans and common laborers. Three black residents of Milwaukee had property valued at $1,000 or more in 1850. In the summer of that year Milwaukee blacks felt secure enough to exercise their only political right, the right to assemble and protest. The occasion was a federal law that allowed Southern slavecatchers to apprehend blacks in the North upon a sworn oath that the person was a runaway. The black was not entitled to judicial process and the magistrate received a higher fee if he sent the black into slavery than if he set the person free. Milwaukee's blacks, although few, if any, were fugitives, instantly recognized the threat to their security. At a mass meeting a black leader warned his people that they risked being sent into slavery unless they stood together and, with help from friendly whites, prevented enforcement of the law. The meeting adopted resolutions pledging "to come forward at any alarm given and rescue our fugitive brethren even unto death." In succeeding months Wisconsin's black community assisted a number of fugitives along the "Underground Railroad" to reach the safety of Canada, but it would be four years before the opportunity arose to challenge directly the Fugitive Slave Law.

▼

Anti-Slavery Movement

Few among the white people of the North favored the immediate abolition of slavery. Such a move, many feared, would involve the confiscation of Southerners' property and that was too drastic a step for property-conscious Americans. The Constitution was another barrier to abolition. Slavery was protected by state constitutions and laws in the Southern states. Congress had no power under the United States Constitution to alter state laws. Nevertheless, by the 1840s there was a growing feeling that slavery was morally wrong and that something should be done to confine it. The Liberty Party, founded in 1840, reflected this view. It proposed that Congress prohibit slavery in the areas under its jurisdiction, the District of Columbia and the Western territories. The party ran a candidate for president in 1840 and again in 1844, but it received only a few thousand votes, mostly among transplanted Yankees in New York and Ohio. It did, however, manage to elect a few congressmen from those areas, and elsewhere, in districts evenly divided between Whigs and Democrats, the presence of a Liberty Party candidate forced the candidates of the major parties to take a stand on the issue of slavery.

The War with Mexico in 1846 brought to a head the question of slavery in the West. Many Northerners suspected that the war was part of a Southern plot to extend slave territory in the region between Texas and California. From 1846 to 1848 Northerners in Congress repeatedly attempted to prohibit slavery in the land acquired from Mexico by the war. The discussion gave rise to a new form of anti-slavery known as "Free Soil." The idea of the Free Soilers was to ignore slavery where it was already entrenched and work instead to prevent the expansion of the institution into the Western territories. The proposal was moderate enough to attract a broad following; it was the lowest common denominator of anti-slavery feeling. It also appealed to the prejudices of the North because it confined blacks to the states of the old South and kept them out of the Western settlements. In the presidential election of 1848 the Liberty Party was reincarnated as the Free Soil Party.

The Liberty Party had substantial support in the Wisconsin counties settled by Yankees and it maintained a newspaper in Milwaukee, the *American Freeman*. In 1848, just 10 days before Wisconsin was admitted to the Union, Sherman Booth, a 35-year-old native of western New York, arrived to take over the paper. A universal reformer, whose views on temperance were as fanatical as his views on slavery, Booth was erratic and abrasive, but for the next decade he almost singlehandedly dominated the slavery debate in Wisconsin. Wisconsin gave its electoral vote to the Democratic candidate in 1848, but the

Sherman Booth.

candidate of the Free Soil Party (ex-president Martin Van Buren) received 27 percent of the popular vote, a better showing than he obtained in any other state except Massachusetts.

The Fugitive Slave Law of 1850 was part of the Great Compromise that admitted California to the Union as a free state. The three-man Wisconsin delegation in the House of Representatives—a Democrat, a Whig and a Free Soiler—voted in favor of the admission of California and against every other feature of the compromise. The compromise nevertheless slipped through, as moderates in both North and South hoped it would end the agitation over slavery. In Wisconsin it did nothing of the sort. Meetings were held all over the state to protest the Fugitive Slave Law. Southern insistence on including the law in the compromise package proved a ruinous mistake, for the law carried slavery into the North. What had been an abstract moral issue suddenly became personal. Slavery was no longer a "peculiar institution" in a distant state—it was a black face peering out from prison bars asking for help. Sherman Booth called on all persons "with a human heart in their bosoms" to defy the law. A gathering in Winnebago County resolved: "The Fugitive Law has no binding force upon us and therefore we will continue, as heretofore, to help the slave escape." It would nevertheless be four years before the tension between law and liberty was put to the test.

▼

Challenging the Fugitive Slave Law

It was the spring of 1854. The nation's attention was riveted on Washington, D.C., where Steven A. Douglas, senator from Illinois, was steering through Congress a bill to create two new territories in the Great Plains, Kansas and Nebraska. In Wisconsin, on a March evening, a deputy federal marshal and three associates entered a shack about four miles north of Racine where Joshua Glover, a runaway slave, was playing cards with two other black men. After a sharp struggle, the marshal bludgeoned Glover, put him in manacles and carried him away in a wagon.

The next morning the mayor of Racine sent a telegram to Booth asking him to find out if a warrant had been issued for Glover's arrest. Booth learned from the federal district judge that Glover's master had obtained a warrant in accordance with the Fugitive Slave Law and that Glover was lodged in the Milwaukee jail. When the judge refused Booth's request for an open trial of the fugitive, Booth mounted his horse and, "full-bearded, bald-headed and in trumpet tones, riding through the principal streets," shouted: "Freemen, to the rescue." He also called for a meeting in the courthouse square. A crowd of several thousand assembled and demanded Glover's release on a writ of habeas corpus. At that juncture, the Racine County sheriff, backed by a hundred men, appeared with a warrant for the arrest of the deputy marshal on a charge of assault and battery on Glover. With the law now on the side of liberty, the lawless took charge. The mob made a rush for the jailhouse door, broke it with a huge timber, and set Glover free. He was spirited by night to Racine and put on a boat to Canada.

Booth, who received more credit for the incident than he perhaps deserved, was not made of the stuff of martyrs. He denied having inflamed the mob and insisted that he was only trying to find Glover a good lawyer. Nevertheless, he was arrested on a federal charge of violating the Fugitive Slave Law and abetting an escape. He was jailed briefly and fined $1,000. Over the next few years Booth would be at the center of a major confrontation between the state of Wisconsin and the federal government.

In the meantime, Booth had a new cause—the Kansas-Nebraska Act. Steven A. Douglas had viewed the new territories as a testing ground for his solution to the problem of slavery, "popular sovereignty." The idea was to remove the issue from the halls of Congress and place it in the hands of the people directly involved, the residents of the Western territories. Let them choose between slavery and free soil! Douglas was confident that the pioneers of the plains, an area not fit for cotton cultivation, would vote themselves free and that would end the matter. Unfortunately for Douglas, he failed to reckon upon the growing suspicion of a "slave power conspiracy."

In order to ensure a genuine choice for the voters, Douglas had to incorporate an amendment to his bill that repealed the Missouri Compromise of 1820, which had declared the region between the Mississippi River and the Rocky Mountains north of 36 degrees 30 minutes latitude to be free territory. This move violated a fundamental tenet of Washington, Jefferson, Madison and other Founding Fathers that slavery was an evil and should be confined to a tiny part of the country until it collapsed of its own weight. To many outraged Northerners Douglas had opened the entire West to the potential for slavery. No one worried much about Nebraska, but Kansas was another matter. It lay directly to the west of Missouri, a slave state, and was almost certain to be populated by a number of Southern sympathizers. To men like Sherman Booth, the Kansas-Nebraska Act was the product of an insidious conspiracy to bolster slavery by letting it invade virgin lands.

▼

Birth of the Republican Party

Even before the act cleared the two houses of Congress, meetings were being held all over the North and there was talk of a new political party made up of the remnants of the fading Whig Party, plus anti-Nebraska Democrats and Free Soilers. On the last day of February, while the bill was still under Senate debate, a meeting was held at the Congregational church in Ripon, Fond du Lac County. The meeting, which was attended by women as well as men, resolved that if the Nebraska bill passed, the old parties would be dissolved and a new party formed on the basis of anti-slavery. The organizer of the meeting, Alan E. Bovay, a New York-born lawyer, proposed the name Republican for the new party because it suggested "equality" and had been "used by the party of Jefferson in its best and purest days." Most important, thought Bovay, "in point of expediency," Republican was "the cherished name with our foreign population of every nationality." On June 15, after the Kansas-Nebraska had been voted into law, Horace Greeley, the nation's most prominent journalist, endorsed the named Republican in his *New York Tribune.*

On July 13 more than a thousand delegates, many of them arriving on the newly opened railroad from Milwaukee, poured into Madison for a convention to organize the new political party. Although the meeting attracted enthusiastic amateurs from all parts of the state, experienced Whig and Free Soil politicians controlled the proceedings. The convention resolved: "That we accept this issue [freedom or slavery] forced upon us by the slave power and in the defense of freedom will cooperate and be known as Republicans." The convention chose a central committee and adjourned amidst resounding cheers. Conventions throughout the North set up similar organizations. The new party attracted religious-minded reformers of all stripes, including temperance advocates and nativists who wanted to stop the influx of foreign immigrants. In Wisconsin, however, the party concentrated on anti-slavery and avoided any mention of temperance or nativism that might alienate the immigrant vote. The tactic worked. In the fall election of 1854 Republicans elected two of Wisconsin's three congressmen and won a majority in the State Assembly. Meeting in January 1855, the Assembly chose a Republican to the United States Senate. Later that year it could expect to elect a governor as well. Only in neighboring Michigan was the new-found party so quickly and so brilliantly successful.

In the first territorial elections in Kansas, Missourians crossed the border and voted illegally, thus putting in office a proslavery legislature. President Franklin Pierce, a Democrat, recognized the legislature as legitimate and sent a pro-Southern governor to Kansas. Northerners, seeing in these events further evidence of a Southern conspiracy, resolved to populate Kansas with free farmers. In Boston, the Massachusetts Emigrant Aid Society talked loudly of sending guns as well as voters to Kansas. (It actually sent precious little of either.) In March 1856 a group of prominent Republicans held a mass meeting in Milwaukee to organize the Kansas Emigrant Aid Society of Wisconsin. The society raised funds, recruited emigrants and sent an agent to Kansas to look over the land. A Ladies' Kansas Aid Society sponsored a concert and a dinner to raise money, and it organized sewing circles to make clothing for emigres. Within a few weeks a well-equipped train of 55 wagons and several hundred pioneers, who had gathered from all over the state, left Milwaukee for Kansas and in the fall another expedition set out. The Wisconsinites joined other Free Soilers in settling in the Lawrence/Topeka area, about 50 miles up the Kansas River and outside the Missourians' sphere of influence. The emigrants' letters home, telling of skirmishes with Missouri "border ruffians" and expressing a determination to build a free Kansas, kept the slavery issue burning in Wisconsin politics.

In the presidential election of 1856 Wisconsin voters cast 66,090 ballots for the Republican candidate, John C. Fremont, and 52,843 for the Democratic candidate, James Buchanan. Republicans elected all three of the state's congressmen and they won large majorities in both houses of the Legislature. In early 1857 the Legislature elected a second Republican to the United States Senate. Another Republican, Alexander Randall, was elected governor that year. Elected lieutenant governor was the German political refugee, Carl Schurz, whom party leaders had added to the ticket in an overt effort to appeal to the German vote. Even Schurz's revolutionary activity was seen as a plus. Sherman Booth reminded the Republican convention that the state was defying the federal government in the matter of the Fugitive Slave Law. As a result, "the idea of Schurz being a revolutionist rather pleased us and we thought if he was a red Republican and we had all been stigmatized as black Republicans, he would answer our purpose very well!" Republicans would control the state for the next 17 years.

▼

Sounding the Alarm

The mob action that freed Joshua Glover did not end the confrontation between Wisconsin and the federal government over the Fugitive Slave Law. In fact, it was but the first act of the drama. Federal authorities arrested Sherman Booth on charges of having obstructed enforcement of the law, and he was sentenced to jail. But the Wisconsin Supreme Court issued a writ of habeas corpus freeing him from the jurisdiction of the federal courts on grounds that the Fugitive Slave Law, under which he had been indicted and convicted, was unconstitutional. Twice more federal authorities jailed Booth and each time the state Supreme Court set him free. In effect, the Supreme Court was asserting the authority to review the constitutionality of a federal law and to nullify the statute when it failed to meet the test. In 1857 the Republican Legislature joined several other Northern states in enacting a "personal liberty law," which guaranteed the right of habeas corpus to persons detained as fugitive slaves and prohibited the use of any state agency in the recovery of fugitives.

In May 1857 the United States Supreme Court entered the arena with some judicial legislation of its own. The occasion was a law suit instituted by a slave named Dred Scott. Scott claimed his freedom by virtue of having resided with his master, an Army surgeon, in parts of the Louisiana Purchase that had been declared free soil by the Compromise of 1820. Speaking for a divided court,

Chief Justice Roger B. Taney declared the Missouri Compromise unconstitutional and dismissed Scott's plea on grounds that he had never resided on free soil. Congress had no power to restrict slavery, Taney declared, because to do so would be to deprive Southerners of their property rights without due process, in violation of the Fifth Amendment to the Constitution.

The import of this decision was to stand the nation's Founding Fathers on their heads. Washington, Jefferson and Madison, all slaveowners themselves, had sought to confine the "peculiar institution" to a few states of the Old South, leaving the rest of the nation free. The Dred Scott decision made slavery a national institution, with the realm of freedom confined to a few Northern states, where it was protected by state laws and constitutions. To many in Wisconsin it seemed that the "slave power" had reached out anew. It had long controlled Congress and the White House; now its insidious tentacles were reaching into the Supreme Court. What ground was left for freedom?

Abraham Lincoln, a Republican politician little known outside his home state of Illinois, had an inspired answer. The year 1858 was another election year for Congress and among the seats at stake was that of Illinois Senator Steven A. Douglas. With little hope of unseating the powerful Douglas, Illinois Republicans placed Lincoln, who had served a single term in Congress more than a decade earlier, on the sacrificial altar. In his speech accepting the party's nomination, Lincoln evoked the Biblical phrase, "A House Divided Against Itself Cannot Stand." His alarmed audience thought he was predicting Civil War. Instead, he was sounding the alarm against the advance of slavery. The divided house cannot stand, he said; instead "It must become all one thing or all the other." And he thought the tendency was toward a nation of slaves. Lincoln was addressing a larger constituency—the factory workers in Chicago and the wheat farmers in Illinois' black earth prairie. Slavery, Lincoln was implying, was not a local institution peculiar to the South, nor was it necessarily confined to blacks. (A decade earlier Karl Marx in Germany had talked of the "wage slavery" of workers under a capitalist system.) Slavery, said Lincoln, was a threat to all. His plea was to the lower economic rungs of Northern society. In time Lincoln's rhetoric would give the Republicans a strong farmer/laborer constituency, much in the tradition of Thomas Jefferson and Andrew Jackson.

Lincoln's rhetoric would eventually win the hearts of the German and Irish voters of Wisconsin, who had resisted the earlier overtures of Republicans. In the meantime Wisconsin carried on its own "civil war" with the federal government. Sidestepping the Wisconsin Supreme Court, S.V.R. Ableman, the federal marshal in Milwaukee—and at 300 pounds a man not accustomed to resistance—sued in federal court in Washington, D.C., for the custody of Sherman Booth, whom the federal district court in Wisconsin had convicted. Booth refused to appear in Washington or be represented by counsel, submitting instead a pamphlet declaiming the unconstitutionality of the Fugitive Slave Law. The United States Supreme Court issued a writ of error to the Wisconsin Supreme Court and demanded the records of its proceedings. The Wisconsin court refused, silently reasserting its independence of federal authority.

On March 7, 1859, Chief Justice Taney announced the decision of the Supreme Court in the case of *Ableman v. Booth*. He reversed the decision of the Wisconsin court, affirmed the validity of the Fugitive Slave Law and ordered the marshal to rearrest Booth. The Wisconsin court capitulated and denied Booth a writ of habeas corpus, but he remained at liberty, apparently because no one was willing to incarcerate him. Booth was at the height of his political influence. The Republican Legislature, with support from Governor Randall, passed resolutions declaring the Supreme Court's "arbitrary act of power" to be "void and of no force" in the sovereign state of Wisconsin.

Booth was also at the end of the line politically. In April 1859 he was indicted for having seduced the 14-year-old daughter of a neighbor and having an "illicit connection" with her. Although Booth was acquitted by a divided jury, his moral authority was gone. And it was only the beginning of his legal troubles. The owner of Joshua Glover obtained a judgment against him of $1,000, which forced him to sell his printing press and declare bankruptcy. Sherman Booth had 43 years of life remaining, but he had written *finis* to his mark on history.

Wisconsin's five-year confrontation with the federal government reflected the "radicalism"* of Wisconsin Republicans, and in turn it intensified their sense of purpose. As a result, Lincoln was not their first choice when the Republican presidential nominating convention assembled in Chicago in May 1860. During his famed debates with Douglas in 1858 Lincoln had repeatedly stressed his commitment to Free Soil; he insisted that he had no interest in emancipating slaves or ensuring their legal rights. Wisconsin delegates instead favored the New Yorker William H. Seward, former Whig leader whose commitment to anti-slavery dated back to the 1840s. Nevertheless, on the third ballot, when a vote switch gave Lincoln a narrow majority, Carl Schurz, leader of the Wisconsin delegation, seconded a motion to make the nomination unanimous.

During the campaign Wisconsin's Republican newspapers adopted the theme set forth by Lincoln in his "House Divided" speech, stressing that Republicans supported "the interests of free rather than slave labor," the rights of white men rather than black. They also echoed the ideas of Senator James R. Doolittle, a former Democrat blessed with a gift for oratory and little else, who advocated the return of blacks to Africa. Colonization was the oldest of anti-slavery arguments and the most deceptive because it involved getting rid of blacks, not slavery. (The American Colonization Society, founded in 1817, had financed the transport of several hundred blacks to western Africa, all of them free.) By emphasizing the removal of blacks, rather than slavery, Wisconsin Republicans hoped to broaden their popular base, particularly among the foreign-born, who did not want to compete with free blacks in the labor market. Carl Schurz, a member of the party's national committee, took charge of its "foreign department." He toured New York, Pennsylvania, Indiana, Illinois and Missouri before returning to Wisconsin for the final effort.

The result, as to the ethnic vote, was mixed. German Protestants

* "Radical Republicans" were those who were ahead of Lincoln and other "Free Soilers" on the question of emancipating slaves.

did move into Republican ranks, while Catholics adhered to the Democratic Party. Irish Catholics also remained Democratic. Norwegians were likewise divided. One explained that his community was not "well-informed enough to judge which of [the candidates] are right," but it voted for the "Southern Democrat" anyway. That community of Norwegians in fact voted for Steven A. Douglas, candidate of the Northern wing of the divided Democratic Party. The Republicans' central constituency—persons born in America or England—knew what they were about, nevertheless. Lincoln won the state by 86,116 ballots to 66,063 for all other candidates combined.

▼

War Looms

A month after Lincoln was elected, South Carolina seceded from the Union, hoping to trigger a chain reaction among other Southern states. The gamble paid off; by the end of January 1861 the states of the lower South, from Georgia to Texas, had walked out of the Union. In February a convention in Montgomery, Alabama, drafted a constitution for the Confederate States of America and elected Jefferson Davis president of the new "nation." In Washington, James Buchanan watched helplessly as the final minutes of his presidency ticked away.

In the weeks before Lincoln's inauguration on March 4 Congress worked frantically at a compromise that would appease the South. As the price of union, Southerners demanded nothing less than constitutional amendments that would impose slavery on the territories and guarantee the right to hunt down fugitives. Although some Northern congressmen were willing to appease the South, the Wisconsin delegation would have none of it. Cadwallader C. Washburn of Mineral Point, who had been elected in 1856, made himself the spokesman for no-compromise Republicans throughout the North. He claimed that the attack on the "personal liberty laws" enacted by the Northern states was "a mere excuse for long meditated treason." The Constitution, he thought, "needs to be obeyed rather than amended." Taking the floor in the House of

Representatives, he urged Republicans not to retreat. "Let us have disunion," he declared, "and, if need be, civil war rather than dishonor." Lincoln himself rejected any sort of compromise and the congressional session expired without further action.

Although opposed to appeasement, Lincoln had no plan for preserving the Union when he took the presidential oath on March 4, 1861. But a looming crisis did require some sort of action. Federal military bases were located in some of the states that had seceded. By the time Lincoln entered office the military had abandoned all but one, Fort Sumter, guarding the entrance to the harbor of Charleston, South Carolina. The fort had to be supplied or abandoned. Realizing that yielding the fort meant a tacit recognition of the legitimacy of the Confederacy, Lincoln decided to supply it with provisions. He would not reinforce it, however, and he so informed President Davis. On April 13, with Northern supply ships on the way, Southern guns opened fire on the fort. After a day-long bombardment the garrison surrendered. Realizing that war was at hand, but unsure how long it would last, President Lincoln issued a proclamation calling on the states to supply the government with 75,000 men to serve for three months.

▼

Wisconsin Goes to War

On April 15, 1861, Governor Randall received a telegram from Washington asking Wisconsin to supply one regiment of militia, totaling 780 men. Randall promptly wired his assurance that the call would be "promptly met and further calls when made." Earlier that year, in anticipation of a presidential request for troops, the Legislature had appropriated $100,000 for uniforms and equipment and sanctioned a $200,000 war loan. Although the state constitution prohibited the state from going into debt, it did permit borrowing for military defense. Patriotic meetings all over the state encouraged volunteering and pledged financial support. Within one week Governor Randall was able to wire Washington that a regiment of 10 companies was enrolled and officered, awaiting orders. After meeting with other Western governors in early May, Randall wrote the president asking that he call 300,000 men into the field in order to keep the Ohio and Mississippi rivers open for Western trade. Lincoln had already anticipated him. On May 3 he issued a call for 40 regiments of volunteers to serve for three years or the duration of the war. Lincoln was preparing for a good fight and a long one.

By the end of the year Wisconsin had raised 13 regiments of infantry and a company of cavalry, totaling 14,002 men. The figure represented about 9 percent of the white males of military age in the state. This was a higher proportion of the population than has ever stepped forward in the first year of any war the United States has fought. One can only explain the patriotic fervor in terms of the years of prewar tension. Southern aggressiveness, its seeming takeover of the national government, its disdain for the ideals of the Founding Fathers—important, at least, to native-born Americans—had led Northerners to feel that they were victims of an insidious conspiracy, behind which was something vaguely known as the

Old Abe and the Color Guard of the Eighth Wisconsin.
Photograph by an unknown soldier after the fall of Vicksburg in July 1863.

"slave power." The impulse to volunteer stemmed from hatred of things Southern, not necessarily hatred of slavery. Most Wisconsinites reprobated slavery in principle, but few had any sympathy for black people. Indeed, Wisconsin soldiers exhibited a bias toward blacks throughout the war.

The volunteers far exceeded the president's initial request, and after the first regiment formed in Milwaukee, there were 20 companies of men left over. Instead of disbanding them, as the secretary of war suggested, Governor Randall assembled them at the fairgrounds outside of Madison owned by the State Agricultural Society. The colonel of the first regiment to be formed there, the Second Wisconsin (one of the most famous regiments of the war) named the site Camp Randall. It became the mustering grounds of the state; by the end of the war some 70,000 recruits obtained their "basic" training at Camp Randall.

The only restrictions on volunteering were racial. Both state and federal authorities were determined that the Northern army be lily white. When Governor Randall issued his first call for militia in April 1861, a leading black citizen of Madison, W.H. Noland, wrote to inquire whether the governor would accept a company of black soldiers. Many of his race, Noland explained, were eager to "hurl back" the accusation that they were "neither brave or loyal and not reliable in an emergency like the present." Randall turned him down. He also turned down a white company commander, who offered the service of 200 Menominees, "all well armed with rifles, sure at forty rods." The next year, Randall's successor, Edward Salomon, telegraphed Lincoln's secretary of war: "I am applied to by parties who offer to raise a battalion or more of friendly Indians in this State: also one or more companies of colored citizens." The secretary promptly replied: "The President declines to receive Indians or negroes as troops."

For many a Wisconsin farmboy the trip to Madison for training was his first adventure into the world beyond his horizon. He departed home "with bands playing, banners flying and people shouting" and received new ovations at every stop along the way. The Eau Claire Eagles distinguished their regiment by carrying a live eagle as their mascot (later to be famous as "Old Abe"), but their itinerary was typical. They marched down to the Chippewa River where a steamboat took them to La Crosse. From there they went by train to Madison. One young man, experiencing his first train ride, described it thus: "I was afraid we were off the track every time we crossed a switch or came to a river. At the towns, girls swarmed on the platforms to ask the boys for their pictures and to kiss the best looking ones."

The Sixth Wisconsin (another famous regiment) was not an imposing sight as it journeyed to Madison from the Baraboo-Reedsburg area. One of the company commanders observed: "The men stumbled along in two ranks, kicking each other's heels. ... A few wore broadcloth and silk hats, more the red shirts of raftsmen, several were in country homespun, one had on a calico coat and another was looking through a hole in the drooping brim of a straw hat. ... The men carried every variety of valise and every species of bundle, down to one shirt tied up in a red handkerchief."

After only a few weeks' training in the use of a firearm and some marching drill, the Wisconsin regiments were sent to war. Most joined the army commanded by General Ulysses S. Grant, operating along the Tennessee and Cumberland rivers. After opening these rivers by the capture of Confederate forts in February, 1862, Grant marched south along the Tennessee River to the border of Mississippi, using the waterway as a supply line. There in April, near Shiloh Church (or Pittsburg Landing, as the battle was called in the North), Grant fought the first truly vicious battle of the war. The losses were about equal, but Grant could claim victory when the Confederates abandoned the field and retreated after the fighting ceased. For the Wisconsin regiments it was their first blooding and they fought well. The Eau Claire Eagles (the Eighth), according to its general, consisted of "big burly fellows, who could march a mule off its feet," and who proved in the battle "that they could *fight* as well as march." Old Abe celebrated the victory by "whirling and dancing on his perch." The Fourteenth, said one commander, was "the regiment to rely upon in every emergency; always cool, steady and vigorous." The Seventeenth was made up of Irishmen, who led a bayonet charge with the Gaelic battle cry "Faugh a ballagh" ("Clear the way!"). Their proud commander credited them with "the most glorious charge in the campaign."

That summer a total of six Wisconsin regiments served with the Army of the Potomac under General George B. McClellan. Three of them—the Second, Sixth and Seventh—were combined with the Nineteenth Indiana to form the only all-Western brigade in the Army of the Potomac. Their commander devised a distinctive, plumed black hat, which the men wore instead of the kepi favored by both armies. Confederates soon learned to respect "those damned Black Hats." At South Mountain in August 1862, a fight that opened the Second Bull Run campaign, the Black Hat Brigade stumbled upon Stonewall Jackson's corps, which lay hidden on a wooded hilltop awaiting the arrival of Robert E. Lee's army. Although the Southerners lay in the cover of a woods and a railroad embankment, the Black Hats drove without flinching into the storm of gunfire. Watching them advance, General McClellan remarked: "They must be made of iron." The brigade lost 25 percent of its men in the battle. At Antietam a few weeks later, the Sixth

Charge of the Fifteenth Wisconsin at Chicamaugua: Death of Colonel Heg. Oil painting by Alfred Thorsen.

Wisconsin led a charge through a strip of wood and into a cornfield to meet the opening salvo of the Confederates. Blue uniform fell alongside grey in hand-to-hand combat. Of 280 Wisconsin men who went into that cornfield only 130 came out. After that battle the name was changed to the Iron Brigade. It was the most famous unit in the Army.

On July 2, 1862, President Lincoln issued a call for 300,000 additional three-year volunteers. Wisconsin's quota was 11,900. The government was now offering a bounty of up to $100 and some Wisconsin counties gave an additional $50. By September enough men had stepped forward to fill 14 new regiments, considerably above what the state had been asked for. (Instead of filtering recruits into old regiments as replacements, the government ineptly created new regiments, thus increasing its losses by throwing all-green units into battle.) Thereafter enlistments lagged, as the horrendous losses of the summer bore in on the public consciousness. The government had threatened conscription if the states failed to meet their quotas. In November Wisconsin's governor, Edward Salomon, ordered the draft to begin in laggard counties, most of which were populated by German and Irish immigrants. The draft provoked rioting in some communities because many immigrants had fled the old country precisely to avoid compulsory military service.

Lincoln's Emancipation Proclamation, issued in September,

Indian recruits being sworn in. The man in the hat is Thomas Bigford of Tayshe-dah, a farmer who served as a local recruiting officer.

converted a war to preserve the Union into a war against slavery, and the new moral tone encouraged enlistments in Yankee/Protestant counties. But German Catholics were unimpressed. Milwaukee's German Catholic newspaper expressed its horror at the prospect of immigrants being "used as fodder for cannons" in an abolitionist war. Under Lincoln's edict, exclaimed the editor, "Germans and Irish must be annihilated, to make room for the Negro."

Wisconsin regiments were in the thick of fighting again in 1863. At Gettysburg the Sixth Wisconsin played a crucial role on the first day in preventing the Confederate capture of the Round Tops, the hills that anchored the Union flank. So heavy were the losses suffered by the Iron Brigade in the battle that it had to be rebuilt afterwards with Eastern regiments and it lost its distinctive character. In the West 10,000 Wisconsinites accompanied General Grant on his Vicksburg campaign, which cleared the Mississippi River for union warships and cut the Confederacy in two.

In November the Twenty-Fourth Wisconsin was among General William T. Sherman's troops investing the rail center of Chattanooga. The Twenty-Fourth and other regiments were ordered to capture the Confederate rifle pits at the foot of Missionary Ridge. Instead of stopping there, the assault troops spontaneously chased the Confederates to the top of the ridge. In the vanguard was the adjutant of the Twenty-Fourth, Lieutenant Arthur McArthur, who seized the regimental colors from a fallen comrade and planted then atop the hill. Although only 18 years old, McArthur was promoted from lieutenant to major and put in command of the regiment. (He ended the war a "Boy Colonel.")

Battlefield casualties and lagging enlistments induced Congress to pass a new conscription act in March 1863. The act set up a draft board in each congressional district with authority to make a list of the men available for military duty. A man chosen for duty was allowed to provide a substitute or pay a $300 fee that exempted him from duty. That summer the War Department invited the enlistment of African Americans and soon thereafter they were made subject to the draft. A total of 363 "colored troops" were credited to Wisconsin by the end of the war. Wisconsin's Indians were also allowed to join the Army after 1863 and many responded to the lure of bounties and military pay. Out of a total population of 3,300, the Menominee, Oneida and Stockbridge reservations provided 279 recruits, a larger number than many a white community of similar size.

It was a measure of the state's growing weariness that Governor Salomon became involved in a dispute with the War Department over Wisconsin's quota, claiming that the state had been given insufficient credit for the surplus that it had provided on previous calls. He also demanded that the War Department pay his recruits the same bounty ($302 instead of the usual $100) that it was paying in Ohio and Indiana. Draft-dodging was also on the increase, especially in those counties populated by immigrants. Responding to a special call upon those counties in the fall of 1863, county boards drew 15,000 names. A fifth of the men failed to report and a third found substitutes.

The casualties suffered by Wisconsin soldiers mounted in the campaigns of 1864-65. Eight regiments of raw recruits accompanied Grant on his Wilderness campaign of May-June 1864. The Thirty-Sixth went into action just three weeks after it left Madison and suffered 400 casualties in six days, climaxing with the infamous slaughter at Cold Harbor. Regiments that accompanied Sherman in his march across Georgia from Atlanta to the sea fared somewhat better. Sherman faced no organized opposition and for his men the parade through

Peter D. Thomas, a runaway slave who made it to the lines of the Fifteenth Wisconsin Volunteer Infantry. Allowed to join the Army, he served in the regiment's Company G and fought at Chicamaugua and in other battles. He followed Wisconsin veterans to Beloit after the war and attended school there. He settled in Racine and was elected county coroner.

Georgia and the Carolinas was a lark that enabled them to vent their hatred of the South.

An estimated total of 80,595 individuals from Wisconsin served in the war—51 percent of the males of military age. One in seven failed to return.

▼

The End of Slavery

Upon his presidential inauguration in 1861 Lincoln reiterated the promises he had made during the election campaign: He would not disturb slavery where it was already well-established, he would seek only to prevent its expansion into the West. Even after the fighting began, Lincoln adhered to this position. Lincoln shrewdly realized that a war for preservation of the Union had the best chance of broad popular support. He also could not afford to antagonize the strategically important border slave states that had remained in the Union (Delaware, Maryland, Kentucky and Missouri). As a result, for the first year and a half of the war Lincoln resisted the demands of black leaders and Radical Republicans that he give the war a moral dimension by pursuing a policy of emancipation. By mid-1862 the president and the Republican-controlled Congress were at odds on the issue.

Wisconsin Republicans were similarly divided. When Lincoln floated the idea of freeing the slaves gradually and resettling them outside the country, Senator Doolittle heartily approved of this "colonization" idea. Other Republicans contended that repatriation of blacks was unnecessary because, once freed, blacks would be happy to remain in the South, and those in Wisconsin and elsewhere in the North would "soon leave and go there." Republicans momentarily closed ranks, however, when Lincoln issued his Emancipation Proclamation on September 22, 1862. It quieted the Radicals because it made anti-slavery a war aim. Conservatives did not object because the Proclamation purported to free only those blacks belonging to Southerners in rebellion, i.e., slaves over whom Lincoln had no control.

Democrats were uniformly opposed to freeing any slaves; most of them opposed the war itself. The military reverses early in the war won them some popular support. In the 1862 election the civilian vote leaned toward the Democrats, but the soldier vote enabled Republicans to retain control of the state. Nevertheless, the Democrats' open hostility to the war led to ruin when the North began winning battles in 1863. They were stigmatized as the party sympathetic to the traitorous South. In the presidential election of 1864 the Republican ticket (temporarily calling itself the Union Party) of Abraham Lincoln and Andrew Johnson (a Southern Unionist) carried Wisconsin by a comfortable margin. Republicans also won five of the state's six congressional seats.

The 13th Amendment to the Constitution, approved by Congress in January 1865, prohibited slavery everywhere in the United States. With that, emancipation was no longer an issue, but serious questions remained as to the rights of the former slaves, or "freedmen." Would, for instance, they be given the right to vote and hold office? A related question was what to do with the conquered South? Should it be eased painlessly back into the Union, or should it be made to pay a price? These issues were the source of intense debate in April 1865 when Lincoln was assassinated and Andrew Johnson took the reins of government.

As before, Republicans were divided between radicals and moderates. Radicals, such as Rep. Thaddeus Stevens of Pennsylvania, viewed the Southern states as "conquered provinces" at the mercy of Congress. He wanted to remake the South in the image of the North, a land of small farmers. He would do this by breaking up the great plantations and redistributing the land, so that every freedman received "forty acres and a hut." Radicals also saw the need for federal legislation to preserve the rights of the freedmen, the most fundamental of which was the right to vote. Moderate Republicans, including presidents Lincoln and Johnson, wanted to ease the South back into the Union as quickly and pain-lessly as possible, cooperating, if necessary, with the old planter leadership. Black people, they felt, having been freed, could take care of themselves. Lincoln's abhorrence of slavery, it must be remembered, stemmed not from any humanitarian concern for the plight of black people, but from his commitment to "free labor," white as well as black.

Wisconsin Republicans, with the exception of the fence-straddler Senator Doolittle, generally favored federal protection of the rights of the freedmen, though they shied away from the land-appropriation schemes of Thaddeus Stevens. Any disagreements among themselves evaporated when President Johnson tactlessly vetoed a succession of civil rights bills in the spring of 1866. With support from Wisconsin Republicans, Congress sidestepped the president and enshrined civil rights in the federal Constitution, through the 14th Amendment in June 1866.

In their contest with President Johnson, Radical Republicans benefited from lingering memories of the bloody conflict and the desire of many Northern families for revenge. In Wisconsin, no one was more adept at playing on these themes than Lucius Fairchild, who was to become the state's first three-term governor (1866-1872). A veteran who had lost an arm at Gettysburg, Fairchild campaigned in 1865 as the soldier's friend, promising generous benefits to all vet-

Gov. Lucius Fairchild, soldier-politician with the "empty sleeve." Oil painting by John Singer Sargent.

erans and preference in political appointments. Since nearly half of Wisconsin's voting-age men had worn a uniform, it was a flawless strategy. Fairchild was also a master at keeping alive wartime hatreds, a campaign technique known as "waving the bloody shirt." In his inaugural address, his empty sleeve conspicuous, Fairchild spoke of the nobility of sacrifice in the cause of the nation. He denounced secession as treason and called for the hanging of Jefferson Davis. In later elections he referred to the veterans' "fears of another civil war" should Democrats win, and he insisted that another rebellion could be prevented only by maintaining the Republicans in power.

Such rhetoric in Wisconsin and elsewhere in the North paid off handsomely in the fall elections of 1866. Inflamed by Republican oratory and shocked by President Johnson's own political ineptitude, the voters utterly repudiated the president and his approach to reconstructing the South. The new Congress would be dominated by Republican Radicals, who would impose military rule on the South and give the freedmen the vote.

Over the next two years the Wisconsin congressional delegation, with the exception of Senator Doolittle, was a solid phalanx in favor of the Reconstruction Acts of 1867, the impeachment of President Johnson and the 15th Amendment, which extended the suffrage to black males. In the spring of 1868 Johnson survived the Senate vote on his removal from office by a single vote. Among the seven Republicans who helped to save the president was Wisconsin's Doolittle, although the state's Republicans had long since ceased to consider him a party member. In the fall presidential election the Republican candidate Ulysses S. Grant easily carried the state.

▼

Political Shifts

The national Republican Party seemed to lose its sense of purpose in the early 1870s. President Grant watched helplessly as white supremacy organizations in the South, such as the Ku Klux Klan, intimidated blacks and prevented them from voting. One by one the former Confederate states fell under the control of white conservative Democrats. The black population, for the most part, remained tenant farmers, raising cotton on the ex-master's land, in return for a share of the crop. The failure of Reconstruction revealed the limits of the Republican self-help gospel. Republicans had set the blacks free, but failed to find them land or provide the training that they needed to survive in a competitive world.

Wisconsin Republicans also seemed to lose their bearings in the 1870s. Apparently realizing that the party could not subsist forever on the distribution of benefits to veterans, Gov. Fairchild took up the cause of internal improvements. These included river and harbor improvements on Lake Michigan, construction of the long-dreamt Fox-Wisconsin canal and the building of railroads into the pine woods of the Northwest. Since the state was constitutionally forbidden to go into debt for such works, the undertaking required federal grants. The task of obtaining federal monies fell principally upon Rep. Philetus Sawyer of Oshkosh. Impelled by a dream of a Fox River canal that would turn Oshkosh into a great inland seaport, Sawyer had worked hard on obtaining funds for that and other Wisconsin projects since entering Congress in 1865. He remained in the House of Representatives for a decade, during which Wisconsin annually received a disproportionate share of the federal largesse. How much Sawyer's activities benefited the state is hard to say. The railroads that did make their appearance were built mostly with private funds. The great ship canal he wanted never materialized and the funds for river and harbor dredging disappeared into the murky waters of the "improvements." What can be said is that Republicans like Sawyer were no longer motivated by the high ideals of Lincoln and the early standard-bearers of the party. The gospel of free labor and self help had yielded to raw greed at the public trough. Nor were Republican leaders any longer concerned about the welfare of farmers and factory workers. Entrepreneurs and speculators, industrialists, bankers and railroad men were their new clientele.

The same was true, sadly, of the Democrats in the period after the Civil War, although of them it can at least be said that they had few ideals to lose. When the party revived in the 1870s, it was led by wealthy conservatives, sometimes called "Bourbons," after the

French royal family who were overthrown repeatedly by revolution, yet remained devoted to kingly rule, remembering everything and learning nothing. In 1873 the voters rejected both of the major political parties and installed in office a coalition of reformers. It made little difference, for the reformers' agenda was washed away by the financial panic of 1873 and the onset of a great depression. The ensuing years would be ones of slow economic growth and political stagnation.

▼

Travelers' Guide
Settlement

Chippewa Valley Museum, Carson Park, Eau Claire; (715) 834-7871. Exhibits and the restored Anderson Log House chronicle the region's early settlement.

City of Cedarburg, Highway 57, Ozaukee County; (414) 377-9620. Dozens of stone, brick and frame buildings built in the 1840s and '50s form the Washington Avenue Historic District.

Hanchett-Bartlett Homestead, 2149 St. Lawrence Ave., Beloit; (608) 365-7835. Restored 1857 farmstead.

Hawk's Inn, 426 Wells St., Delafield; (414) 646-2140. 1844 stagecoach inn.

Kemper Center, 6501 Third Ave., Kenosha; (414) 657-6005. Complex of mid-1800s historic buildings.

Lincoln-Tallman House, 440 N. Jackson St., Janesville; (608) 752-4519. 1857 Italianate villa.

Little Norway, Highway JG west of Mt. Horeb; (608) 437-8211. 1856 farm buildings and a collection of Norwegian antiques.

Milton House Museum, 18 S. Janesville St., Milton; (608) 868-7772. This 1844 stagecoach inn was a station on the Underground Railroad.

Milwaukee County Historical Center, 910 N. Old World Third St., Milwaukee; (414) 273-8288. Exhibits and a film on the county's pioneer history.

Milwaukee Walking Tours. For brochures describing self-guided tours through Milwaukee's historic neighborhoods, contact the Greater Milwaukee Convention & Visitors Bureau; (800) 231-0903.

Norskedalen Nature and Heritage Center, County PI northeast of Coon Valley; (608) 452-3424. Norwegian heritage museum and pioneer homestead.

Octagon House, 919 Charles St., Watertown; (414) 261-2796. One of the largest pre-Civil War houses in Wisconsin. Also on grounds is the building where the nation's first kindergarten was started in 1856.

Old World Wisconsin, Highway 67 south of Eagle; (414) 594-2116. An outdoor museum, operated by the State Historical Society, showcasing more than 50 immigrant-built structures. Costumed guides demonstrate shearing, spinning, cooking and other pioneer tasks.

Ozaukee County Pioneer Village, Highway I two miles south of Waubeka. An architectural park of 18 restored buildings built between 1840 and 1900.

Pinecrest Historical Village, County JJ and Pinecrest Lane, Manitowoc; (414) 684-5110. Twenty-one restored buildings, including Norwegian and German log homes.

Pioneer Log Village and Museum, Highways 23 and 33, Reedsburg; (608) 524-3419. Complex of 11 buildings dating from 1850 to 1865, operated by the Reedsburg Historical Society.

Sheboygan County Museum, 3110 Erie Ave., Sheboygan; (414) 458-1103. Restored 1852 mansion, 1864 log cabin and 1867 cheese factory.

Swiss Historical Village Museum, 612 7th Ave., New Glarus;

(608) 527-2317. Twelve original and re-created buildings, operated by the New Glarus Historical Society.

Wade House and Wesley Jung Carriage Museum, W7747 Plank Rd., Greenbush; (414) 526-3271. 1850s stagecoach inn and carriage collection, operated by the State Historical Society.

Wisconsin Black Historical Society Museum, 2620 W. Center St., Milwaukee; (414) 372-7677. Exhibits on black Americans in Wisconsin.

Wisconsin's Ethnic Settlement Trail, 518 Water St., Sheboygan Falls; (414) 467-0636. Twenty loop tours through Lake Michigan shoreline communities.

Politics and War

Little White Schoolhouse, Blackburn Street, Ripon; (414) 748-4730. Where the Republican Party was founded in 1854.

Oshkosh Public Museum, 1331 Algoma Blvd., Oshkosh; (414) 424-4730. Extensive Civil War collection.

Frank A. Palumbo Civil War Museum, Carthage College, 2001 Alford Park Dr., Kenosha; (414) 552-8520. One of the best private Civil War collections in the country, amassed in the 1930s.

Wisconsin Veterans Museum, 30 W. Mifflin St., Madison; (608) 264-6086. Exhibits on Wisconsin's Civil War soldiers (and soldiers of other wars), including a diorama depicting the Battle of Antietam. An interactive computer display allows visitors to research Wisconsin veterans who served in the Civil War.

Chapter 5

PINEY WOODS AND GREEN PASTURES

Peshtigo, Wisconsin, in 1871 was a booming lumber town that straddled the Peshtigo River, a swift-flowing stream that emptied into Green Bay, six miles to the south. A narrow-gauge railroad connected the town to its port on the bay, where lumber and wood products transshipped to Chicago. William B. Ogden, millionaire developer of Chicago, owned a sawmill and factory that employed most of the men in the town of 1,700. Every working day the factory's lathes turned out 600 wash pails, 170 tubs, 5,000 broom handles, 50 boxes of clothespins, 45,000 shingles, eight dozen barrelheads, 260 paint pails and assorted other wood utensils. On the west bank of the river were a number of retail stores, and the social life of the town centered on a lodge of Good Templars. A Congregational church with lofty spire claimed the skyline on the east side of the river, and a Catholic church was nearly completed on the west side. Along with these indicia of civic pride and permanence was the establishment of a newspaper in June 1871, the *Marinette and Peshtigo Eagle*, which divided its coverage about equally between the two lumbering communities.

The forest around Peshtigo had recently been lumbered, and the woods were strewn with drying branches and other leafy rubble left behind by the avaricious loggers. But the great stands of white pine to the north and east had attracted the attention of the railroads, whose land claims usually paved the way for the logging companies. Peshtigo was soon to have a direct rail link to Chicago, for the Chicago & North Western was building a line from Green Bay to Marinette and Menominee on the Michigan border. Gangs of woodsmen were preparing the right-of-way by slashing through the stands of pine, spruce, cedar and tamarack, making long piles of the debris and setting it afire. On September 9 the *Eagle* reported that "Mulligan's Brigade of choppers, axes in hand, armed and equipped as the railroad authorities direct, 32 strong, rank and file, passed this place on Saturday en route for the north side of the river, to clear the track for the railroad between Peshtigo and Marinette."

The summer of 1871 was unusually hot and dry in northeastern Wisconsin, and the fires set by the railroad construction gangs caused periodic alarms. On September 16 the *Eagle* noted "heavy fires on the northeast of the village in the woods." Mulligan's Brigade had evidently started its work. In the next few days fires destroyed isolated sawmills and farm buildings. On October 7 the *Eagle* reported that "fires are still lurking in the woods around Marinette, ready to pounce upon any portion of the village in the event of favorable wind." The paper's Peshtigo reporter noted that the Good Templars were planning to put on the temperance drama "Ten Nights in a Bar Room," but, despite this sign of community propriety, he wrote ominously, "unless we have rain soon, only God knows how soon a conflagration may sweep this town."

The following day, Sunday, October 8, dawned hot, dry and calm. On Saturday the little railroad that connected the town with its port on Green Bay had brought 200 laborers from Chicago, employed by the North Western to lay track in the wake of the Mulligan Brigade. They had taken over every inn and saloon in town, and by Sunday morning they were pretty well liquored up. They lurched up and down West Front Street, falling off the plank sidewalks and "emitting horrible blasphemies." Nearly everyone else in town had an uneasy feeling of impending doom. In mid-afternoon the air was filled with smoke, and ashes rained upon the village. The Catholic priest, the Rev. Peter Pernin, who conducted masses in both Peshtigo and Marinette, later recalled that he "perceived above the dense cloud of smoke overhanging the earth, a vivid red reflection of immense extent." Then he suddenly heard "a distant roaring, yet muffled sound, announcing that the elements were in commotion somewhere." With the soul healer's sense of survival, he quickly returned to his Peshtigo home, turned his horse loose from its stable, and began digging a trench for his valuables. While he was thus engaged, a frightened parishioner came by to ask, "But if a fire breaks out, Father, what are we to do?" Without hesitation, Pernin replied, "In that case, Madam, seek the river at once." More than 800 residents of the town would perish because they lacked the good father's wit.

Pernin himself almost delayed too long his race for the river. It was 8 o'clock in the evening before he finished putting his linens, books and church ornaments in the trench and covering them with earth. By then the sky was bright red, the distant roar had become thunderous, and the wind was rising rapidly. The fire, which had begun some miles to the southwest of the city, was driven by a cyclonic air mass that had moved in from the Great Plains—the same storm system that fanned the fire that swept the heart of Chicago on that very day. So intense was the fire that hit Peshtigo

An unknown artist's version of the Peshtigo fire.

that it generated its own weather: hot air currents of near-hurricane force. When Pernin started for the river, he was instantly knocked down by the wind. He rose and staggered forward, blinded by smoke and ash, jostled by panicky people, some rushing toward the river, some away from it. In a memoir written more than three years later, he was still able to record vividly the scene at the river:

Arrived near the river, we saw that the houses adjacent to it were on fire, whilst the wind blew the flames and cinders direct-ly into the water. The place was no longer safe. I resolved then to cross to the other side though the bridge was already on fire. The latter presented a scene of indescribable and awful confu-sion, each one thinking he could attain safety on the other side of the river. Those who lived on the east were hurrying toward the west, and those who dwelt in the west were wildly pushing on to the east so that the bridge was thoroughly encumbered with cattle, vehicles, women, children, and men, all pushing and crushing against each other so as to find an issue from it.

Realizing that the bridge would soon collapse, Pernin moved upriver away from it and found deeper water above the dam. He plunged in, along with the wagon carrying his church tabernacle, which he had somehow dragged all the way from his house. He also pushed into the water panic-stricken people who were kneeling on the riverbank, thinking the world had come to an end. Although immersed up to his head, he had to continually splash water on his head to keep his hair from catching on fire. It seemed as if the air itself was ablaze. His narrative continued:

Not far from me a woman was supporting herself in the water by means of a log. After a time a cow swam past. There were more than a dozen of these animals in the river, impelled thith-er by instinct, and they succeeded in saving their lives. The first mentioned one overturned in its passage the log to which the woman was clinging and she disappeared into the water. I thought her lost, but soon saw her emerge from it holding on

*with one hand to the horns of the cow, and throwing water on
her head with the other. ... I was told later that the animal had
swam to shore, bearing her human burden safely with her; and
what threatened to bring destruction to the woman had proved
the means of her salvation.*

The inferno raced on to the northeast toward Marinette and
Menominee. A series of sand hogbacks deflected it away from the
two towns, although burning embers put the torch to a sawmill and
Pernin's other church. The wildfire then leaped across the Menominee River and raced 14 miles into Michigan, turning thousands of
acres of white pine into a desolate wasteland.

Pernin spent four hours in the river before emerging, exhausted,
to spend the rest of the night stretched out on the sand beach.
Although heavy smoke overlay the town in the morning, obscuring
the sun, the extent of the disaster was readily apparent. The drunk-
en railroad workers had crowded into one of the city's hotels to
escape the heat, and the building had turned into a flaming coffin.
People caught in the street when the inferno struck were turned
instantly into ashes. One member of a rescue party marveled to see
what the intense heat could do to the body of a large lumberjack.
"Nothing remained," he recalled, "other than a mere streak of ashes
that would scarce fill a thimble." In all, about 1,200 people died in
the fire, which ravaged 2,400 square miles of Wisconsin and
Michigan. It was the most disastrous forest fire in American history.

▼

The Logging Era

Forest fires and logging went hand in hand because the fires
were fueled mainly by the wooded debris left behind by the lumbermen. Earlier fires were, of course, not unknown, but they rarely
caused much destruction. Whether set by the Indians to enhance
hunting success or caused by lightning, they quickly burned themselves out when they reached the dark, damp primeval forest with
its virtually barren understory. Logging brought sunlight to the forest floor, and with it dryness and tinder, all ready for the match of

the careless axeman or indifferent railroad builder.

Commercial logging had begun in Wisconsin in the 1840s, and it quickly overtook the fur trade as the territory's main source of income. The white pine was the primary target of the lumbermen because it was light, soft and easily worked by carpenters. The advance of the lumbering frontier into Wisconsin coincided with the invention of the "balloon frame" house, so named because of its spindly 2 x 4 studs and 2 x 6 joists, which, due to the uniformity of its parts, could be built quickly and cheaply. Such houses, made almost entirely of pine, became the standard residential construction for the cities of the Midwest and, indeed, remain so today. The pine woods lay north of a line that extended roughly from Manitowoc to Stevens Point and thence to the falls of the Chippewa and St. Croix rivers. The prevalence of white pine in the North Woods varied from one region to another, and often from one acre to the next. Terrain that was high, sandy and dry was often covered by oak, while poorly drained bogs and sloughs were host to red maple, cedar, spruce and tamarack. Foresters loosely designated as pine land any tract of several hundred acres that contained an average of one or two large pines to the acre and which was near a stream of sufficient depth to float the logs.

The logs were brought out of the woods by water—another reason for the preference for pine, which was light and floated easily. Green hardwoods, such as maple and birch, sullenly dragged on the gravelly bottoms of rivers or sank altogether. Aside from the prevalence of pine, the rivers of Wisconsin were the most important factor in the growth of the state's lumber industry. In the east, the Wolf and the Fox reached far into the interior both north and south of Green Bay. Through the 1840s and '50s Oshkosh and Fond du Lac were rivals for the title of lumber capital of the state. Fond du Lac had an early advantage due to its railroad connection with Sheboygan, which gave it access to the Milwaukee and Chicago markets. But Oshkosh ultimately won out because it was closer to the source of logs in the Wolf River Valley. By 1866 it had about 50 saw mills in operation, and it was shipping lumber by water to Green Bay and by rail to Chicago.

The Wisconsin River, the waterway best known to early settlers, was the first pinery in the 1830s. Although its valley, which drained the central third of the state, yielded an immense amount of lumber, it was soon outstripped by the pineries to the east and west. The river was too shallow for steamboats, and the shifting sand bars allowed only small lumber-carrying rafts. Because the river flowed southwest into the Mississippi, the primary market for its lumber was St. Louis, and the mills along its banks could not compete with the mills of La Crosse and Black River Falls, which had access to the vast pinelands drained by the Black, the Chippewa and the St. Croix rivers. The Chippewa Valley alone was an empire in pine. From Eau Claire, the head of steamboat navigation, the river stretched more than a hundred miles to the northern highlands. Lengthy tributaries, such as the Cedar, the Couderay and the Flambeau created a watery handprint another hundred miles wide. It has been estimated that the Chippewa Valley alone contained one-sixth of all the pine timber between the Appalachians and the Rocky Mountains. Although the western watersheds were not fully developed until after the Civil War, the rivers were such prime movers of logs and

White pine was the lumbermen's primary target.

lumber that railroads did not successfully compete in the lumber trade until the 1890s.

The logging camp was a small affair, although it was usually part of a large corporation that managed dozens of camps. It often contained no more than 20 or 30 lumberjacks, a manager, a cook and the cook's helper, or "cookee." From a management standpoint, the most important laborer was the cook, for camp morale depended on an abundant supply of food reasonably well prepared. The basic fare was bread, salt pork and beans. The camp was usually located on a river, its perimeter determined by the distances crew and horses could haul logs by sled. Logging was a winter occupation because the giant trees could be moved only by horse-drawn sled, usually on grooves formed of ice. The work of the lumberjack was perhaps the hardest, most dangerous, and most poorly paid in the country. Lumber companies, operating on credit, paid their workers only when the season was over. The lumberjacks themselves were rivermen, farmers and itinerant laborers, held in place for a season only by their own indebtedness to the company and the severity of the winter.

The life of a lumberjack appealed only to tough or desperate men capable of handling hard labor for long hours. The lumberjack son of a Madison clergyman found that he was not cut out for the life. He had to work from 3 o'clock in the morning, he wrote his brother, until 7 or 9 in the evening,

> *... and then after supper we roll into our soft, downy couch of lousy blankets, and lay and listen to the mocking bird, with music by the entire band, and snoring in seven different languages, mostly imported—professional snores from Germany and Norway, warranted never to miss a note ... while the beautiful odor of wet socks and foot rags is heard in the near distance, and finally fall asleep to slow music, only to be awakened in a few minutes by the melodious voice of the cook singing, "roll out your dead bodies, daylight in the swamp," etc. Then we get up and go to our beautiful and sumptuous repast of fricasseed pork and beans on the half shell with a basin of*

*reduced ice water, flavored with copperas, and called by the low
and uneducated "tea." Such is life in the woods, but for me,
give me six months, twice a year for two years, in Waupun, or
some other place of enjoyment. Well, Ralph, I hope you will
learn some useful trade of usefulness, that will keep you from
ever having to go to the woods.*

The work involved certain specialties, if not skills. The scaler
marked the trees to be felled and determined the number of logs to
be cut from each. The fellers dropped the tree where it could be
most easily worked. By the 1870s the two-man crosscut saw had
generally replaced the axe, doubling the production of a felling crew.
A bucking crew limbed the tree and cut it into 16-foot logs. The
teamster dragged the logs on the snow to a loading area, where they
were piled onto sleds. A crude block and tackle, drawn by horses,
was used to guide the top logs in place, the pile extending anywhere
from 10 to 20 feet high. Horses, oxen, or—by the end of the century—steam engines pulled the laden sleds to the riverbank, where

Cook and "cookee" in the kitchen shanty of a logging camp near Hayward.

the logs were piled to await the spring thaw. An inspector placed the company's logmark on the butt of each log, so the mass of wood could be sorted out and each company claim its own timber when it reached the sawmill.

The log drive began when the snow melted, the river rose, and the current freshened. The rivermen, whose job it was to keep the unruly logs moving and gather up those that had fallen into backwaters and eddies, have often been portrayed in romantic fashion as courageous souls, riding the bobbing logs with a rhythmic sway, deftly stepping from one to another with only a long pike for balance. A contemporary described them as "hard-living, hard-drinking, hard-fighting, blasphemous pioneers," who were picked from

Log jam on the Chippewa River.

the camp crews for their agility and strength. French Canadians allegedly were the best at riding a log through a rapids.

The most dangerous part of a log drive was breaking up a jam. A narrow bend in the river, a rocky stretch or a sudden shallows could cause the logs to go aground and pile up. Because all the logging companies throughout a watershed put their winter's crop in the river about the same time—April and May—a jam, once started, quickly piled up into a stupendous amount of timber. A famous jam on the Chippewa River in 1869 extended for 15 miles with logs piled 30 feet in the air in some places. In 1886 more than 200 men and two steamboats struggled for six weeks to break a jam on the St. Croix River. Small jams could be loosened by teams of river men nudging the logs apart with their steel-edged pikes. Larger jams were broken up by teams of horses who pulled free the logs near the riverbank, leaving an apron in the middle that was gradually broken up by the current.

Each lumber company maintained its own sawmill on the lower reaches of the river. Each mill attempted to extract its own logs from the mass of timber coming downstream, but that created utter confusion and bitter conflicts. A further difficulty was that a log that missed its intended destination could not be recovered, for there was no way to carry logs upstream. The lumbermen devised a system of log exchange, but this involved a great deal of laborious bookkeeping. The solution was a central organization of lumbermen on each river, and this was generally achieved by 1870. In each logging district a company was formed, which constructed extensive works on the stream for handling and sorting the logs. Such works, unfortunately, had to be maneuverable so steamboats and other traffic could use the river. In 1861 James Allen and Levi Pond of Eau Claire solved the problem by designing a fin boom, which utilized the current of the river to push the boom (consisting of a chain of timbers) across the channel. By turning a series of collapsible rudders or fins on the boom, an operator could induce the current to bring the boom back to shore. The device was put to use on every navigable logging stream in the country.

The boom stopped the floating logs and channeled them into a narrow passage flanked by gaps that led to the booms of individual owners. At each of these gaps a workman, using a long pike pole, picked out the logs belonging to his company. Logs destined for mills farther downstream were allowed to pass on to another sorting place. The system was quite efficient. The sorting works of the Black River Improvement Company, for example, could handle a million board feet of logs a day. Even so, every year 10 percent of the timber cut was lost in the bogs and sloughs of the rivers.

In 1843 a boom on the St. Croix River broke and allowed the logs of a lumbering company to escape downriver. The company finally collected them at Stillwater and bound the logs with ropes and chains into four rafts. It sold the rafts in St. Louis at a good price, and the experiment revolutionized the marketing of lumber. Rafting logs all the way to St. Louis was more economical than sending sawn lumber by rail from Eau Claire or La Crosse to Chicago. By 1870 lumbermen had devised a system for brailing, or belting, logs into a raft. A brail, or hollow frame, was formed by binding logs together with chains and rope. The brail was then

A logging train at the turn of the century. The female passengers may be cooks and cleaners from the logging camp. The pails they are carrying suggest a marketing expedition.

filled with floating logs. A standard brail in use on the Mississippi (similar systems were in use on Lake Superior and Lake Winnebago) was 600 feet long and 45 feet wide. Six brails fastened together made up a Mississippi raft, which was pushed downriver by steamboat. The brails could be subdivided into their components for navigating shoals and rapids. A typical raft contained as much as a million board feet of lumber and covered an area of three acres. Just as the lumber from eastern Wisconsin went into the construction of the lake ports, from Buffalo to Chicago, the lumber from western Wisconsin was refined in St. Louis and used to construct frame houses for the prairie farmers of Illinois, Missouri and Iowa, as well as residential housing in the bustling crossroads of Kansas City and Omaha.

▼

Agricultural Revolution

While the lumber industry was transforming the landscape of northern Wisconsin, an agricultural revolution was reshaping the economy of the southern half of the state. At the outset of the Civil War wheat was still the dominant market crop. In response to Southerners who thought the South could go it alone in the world because "cotton is king," the *Wisconsin State Journal* proclaimed: "Wheat is king, and Wisconsin is the center of the Empire!" The state's wheat and flour production, in fact, was second to that of Illinois, but the importance of the crop justified the journalist's hyperbole. Flour milling was the chief manufacturing process in the state, and Milwaukee was the leading center because it was the hub of a railroad network that brought grain to its millstones. It built its first grain elevator for the storage of wheat in 1857. The flour was marketed in the cities of the eastern seaboard, after being transported across the Great Lakes in wooden sailing vessels.

Labor shortages caused by the Civil War encouraged farm mechanization. The most important device was the McCormick reaper, a mower pulled by horses that cut the grain and gathered it in windrows. Though invented nearly 30 years earlier, the mechanical reaper did not become widely used until the Civil War. Its acceptance was also due to new marketing techniques developed by the McCormick Harvester Company of Chicago, including magazine advertising, traveling salesmen and installment credit. Improved methods of reaping created a demand for faster threshing of wheat, and this was met by the ingenuity of Jerome I. Case, a New Yorker who settled in Racine County in 1842. Case designed and built a threshing machine that separated and collected the seed. Specializing in threshing machines, the J. I. Case Company was one of the largest manufacturers of farming machinery in the Northwest when the Civil War broke out, and by 1870 it was one of the largest in the country, with annual sales of threshers and wagons exceeding $1 million.

The steady influx of German and Scandinavian immigrants during the 1860s helped relieve the labor shortage caused by the war, but so did the entry of women into the labor market. In 1864 the editor of the Green Bay Advocate noted proudly: "But we have a great element of strength up here which goes far toward repairing the loss in farm hands by the war. The sturdy, muscular German and Belgian women plough and sow and reap with all the skill and activity of men, and we believe are fully their equals in strength. If need be they will even go into the pineries and do the logging." Women also provided the labor for several new industries that sprang up during or shortly after the war. Among these was the manufacture of beer. Public tastes in alcoholic beverages, influenced, no doubt, by the palates of German and Scandinavian immigrants, shifted during the 1850s and '60s from whiskey to lager beer. A discriminatory wartime tax on whiskey encouraged the trend. The hop vine had been introduced in Wisconsin by emigrants from New York, and in the postwar years a "hop craze" swept through the farms of the southeastern part of the state. Hops were harvested by itinerant workers, most of them young women. The harvest was a gala time, a time of feasting and music, and good wages attracted women from all over the state. One journalist reported:

> *The railroad companies are utterly unable to furnish cars for the accommodation of the countless throngs who daily*

find their way to the depots ... to take the cars for the hop fields. Every passenger car is pressed into service, and freight and platform cars are fixed up as well as possible for the transportation of the pickers. Every train has the appearance of an excursion train, on some great gala day, loaded down as they are with the myriads of bright-faced young girls.

Another alternative to wheat cultivation that became commercially successful during these years was dairy farming. By the 1890s it had supplanted wheat as the state's preeminent source of income.

Wheat was the crop of choice among pioneer farmers because it required relatively little labor. A crop could be harvested in the very first year by sowing seed under trees deadened by girdling. Unlike tobacco, which required constant attention to the condition of leaves and presence of insects, or corn, which had to be weeded frequently, wheat grew with little attention. It did not even require deep plowing. The only labor was at seed-time and harvest. Repeated crops depleted the soil, but so long as land was cheap it mattered little. Pioneers either cleared new land of their own or moved on to the West. William W. Daniells, professor of chemistry and agriculture at the University of Wisconsin, tried in vain to get wheat farmers to mend their ways. Wheat farming, he wrote in 1878, was "mere land-skimming.... It was always taking out of the purse and never putting in." Because the farmer had "every obstacle to contend with except cheap and very fertile land... *poor* farming was the only profitable farming," but it resulted inevitably in exhausted soil and "the habit of loose and slovenly farming." The good professor predicted that change "to a rational method that will preserve the soil's fertility and pay for the labor it demands" would come only "with the replacement of the pioneer farmers by immigrants accustomed to better methods of culture."

The transition that Professor Daniells foresaw was already underway in the late 1870s as the railroads pushed onto the plains of western Minnesota and the Dakotas, opening a vast realm for wheat culture. Wisconsin's Yankee farmers, accustomed to wheat growing, followed the railroads onto the plains; German and Scandinavian immigrants took up their depleted farms. Another University of Wisconsin professor, Frederick Jackson Turner—later famed for his essay, "The Significance of the Frontier in American History"—noticed, on a fishing trip in northern Wisconsin, recent German arrivals "dispossessing whole townships of Americans and introducing the customs and farming methods of the fatherland." European farmers had long been in the habit of restoring their fields with lime and manure, and they were accustomed to working land that was too steep or rocky to submit to the plow. Dairying, with which they were also acquainted, was adaptable to marginal lands— and it was self-restoring.

The first cattle in Wisconsin were of French-Canadian stock brought to the Illinois country in the 18th century to feed the soldiers of frontier outposts. They were spindly animals valued for meat, rather than milk, and even the meat was probably inferior to that of the deer and buffalo available in the wild. "Improved" cattle, bred in England and valued for their milk production, appeared in the Wisconsin Territory in the 1830s. Although many farmers, especially emigrants from New York, kept a cow or two by the 1840s, the milk was consumed at home. Care of the cow was a chore for mother and children, and no effort was made to prolong the lactation period beyond a few months of the spring and summer. A farmer with a modest surplus did not bother to sell his milk because it would have spoiled before his plodding oxen could carry it more than a few miles. Most families churned butter but in a casual and unsanitary way. Nor was there any effort to control what the cow was eating, and many unwholesome odors—from wild onions to wild garlic—found their way into the milk and thence into the butter. Butter that was shipped to urban areas was an amalgam of contributions from many farms, without inspection or quality control. As late as the 1870s Wisconsin butter was sold in Chicago by the hundredweight as a base for wagon-wheel lubricants—in short, as axle grease.

Soil exhaustion and declining yields of wheat in the southeastern counties by the 1860s brought forth a boisterous collection of dairy advocates, most of them emigrants from New York where dairying had replaced wheat culture two decades earlier. Utilizing the state's agricultural journals, they advised farmers to "substitute the plow for the cow." Although German and Scandinavian immigrants were receptive, few could read English, and the Yankee population was determinedly resistant. Governor William Dempster Hoard reflected the exasperation of the reformers when he burst out: "One reason there is so much truth in the oft-reiterated remark—'Farming don't pay'—is that there is not another business on the face of the earth that, in proportion to the numbers engaged in it, supports so many incompetents."

Hoard had begun his career as a dairy farmer and a country journalist who founded *Hoard's Dairyman*, soon to be the nation's preeminent dairy publication. Realizing that quality control was the essence of commercial dairying, Hoard in 1872 helped to organize the Wisconsin Dairyman's Association. The association established a dairy board of trade at Watertown, modeled after one in New York, to bring buyers and sellers together in an auction setting. Competition alone forced the dairymen to mind the quality and

The Alex Smith farm, Bear Creek Valley, near Lone Rock, ca. 1875. The look of a farm before the advent of silos and barbed-wire fencing.

uniformity of their butter and cheese.

Cheesemaking required more knowledge and skill than the making of butter, and it was practiced on a commercial scale only by a handful of farmers, all of them New Yorkers. But cheese also had the most potential for profit. Cheese used the whole milk, rather than just the butterfat, and less wastage brought greater returns. It also traveled better than butter and required less refrigeration. But, as with butter, quality control was the essence of marketing.

The cheese factory was the answer—and the basis of the dairy industry when it finally caught hold. Originating in eastern Europe, the cheese factory was introduced in New York in 1851, and it revolutionized dairying methods there within a decade. The idea invaded Wisconsin in 1864 when Chester Hazen, an emigrant from the Empire State, built a factory at Ladoga in Fond du Lac County. Since good cheesemakers were a rare breed, the cheese factory utilized an economy of skill. It purchased the milk from farmers in the surrounding region, thus consuming the output of 200 to 500 cows. The cheesemaker, usually of New York or German birth, supervised the production of two to 20 factories, and thus ensured a product of uniformly good quality.

Filling a poured cement silo near Waupaca, ca. 1895.

Since even the smallest cheese factory required contributions from at least 200 cows, farmers committed to the new system had to find converts, and the proselytizing was reminiscent of a religious tent-camp meeting. Resistance was not simply a matter of innate conservatism. Cheese production imposed a tyranny of its own because bad milk from one farm could ruin a batch of cheese for an entire district. The discipline required of dairymen as they entered the marketplace was not unlike the discipline being imposed on urban factory workers who found their lives governed by whistles and work rules.

Even with new recruits the cheesemakers' demands always seemed to exceed the supply of milk. The difficulty was winter feed. Because most farmers cut and stored only enough hay to keep their animals alive during the winter months, they made no effort to milk the cows after October. In addition, they assumed that the winter "rest" increased output during the brief milking season, when the cow had its calf. Cheese factories accordingly operated only for four or five months, during what was known as the "flush" season. Larger barns, capable of holding more hay, was one answer, but barns were expensive to build. In 1880 one farm expert estimated that a barn capable of accommodating 30 cows cost about $3,000. Some farmers preferred octagonal barns, which, for less money, could be designed to serve as milking shed, hayloft, carriage house and horse stable.

The most economical solution to the problem of winter forage was the silo. The concept of storing grain in air-tight pits or trenches was known to the Romans (the term "silo" is derived from a Latin word meaning "trench"), but European farmers did not begin experimenting with it until the mid-19th century. German farmers began storing chopped up beets and beet leaves in large wooden receptacles, in a process similar to the way they made sauerkraut for themselves. In 1877 a Frenchman published the results of 25 years of experiments with silage—green feed fermented in a tightly enclosed space, and American farmers undertook experiments of their own. The fermentation process converted the carbohydrates into acids, chiefly lactic acid, which helped to prevent the silage from spoiling. The essence of successful silage was the exclusion of air, that is, oxygen. With too much air the fermentation process heated up and turned the green matter to ash. Any plants, except members of the cabbage family, could be used for silage—corn, oats, grass or beans. The crop had to be chopped finely and pressed tightly into an enclosed space. The first silos were square and made of wood, but these could not withstand the pressure. Later silos were round and made of glazed brick or concrete.

In 1881 Dean William A. Henry of the University of Wisconsin School of Agriculture obtained a legislative appropriation of $4,000 to build an experimental silo on the university farm. The silage was accepted by the university herd, and Dean Henry, joined by editor Hoard, became an apostle for the new feeding system. It was found that a single acre of grain made into silage could feed three cows through the winter, whereas it required hay from two acres to maintain a single cow. The reason was that grass made into hay lost about 50 percent of its nutrient value, while corn made into silage lost only about 10 percent of its nutrients.

The cheese factory and the introduction of the silo completed the dairy revolution. Conservative farmers, to be sure, were slow to accept the new developments. As late as 1904 a statewide census reported only 716 silos in Wisconsin. Nevertheless, by that date the vast majority of Wisconsin farmers were committed to dairy farming.

▼

Growth of the Railroads

Commercial dairying—like the lumber and flour industries of previous decades—depended upon a national, even international market. Lumber and flour had been shipped primarily by water; the dairy industry, requiring swift and frequent delivery of its products, was utterly dependent upon the railroads. William D. Hoard, as in so many other ways, was among the first to see the potential in rail transport. Shortly after forming the Wisconsin Dairymen's Association in 1872 Hoard made inquiries about the refrigerator car developed by Chicago meat-packer Gustavus A. Swift for shipping chilled carcasses to Eastern markets. The early refrigerator cars were cooled by blocks of ice, and this created an additional market for another Wisconsin industry, ice cutting. Lakeside cities, such as Green Bay and Oshkosh, were already recognized centers for large-scale ice production, with markets in the residential areas of Milwaukee and Chicago. The railroads quickly surpassed the residential demand. Before long 12 firms were operating in the Green Bay area, shipping to the Chicago-based railroads a million tons of ice a year.

In addition to obtaining refrigerator cars, the Dairymen's Association was able to negotiate favorable rates with "fast freight" shippers who guaranteed delivery within six days to New York and eight to Boston. Because they had the advantage of cheaper land and labor costs, Wisconsin dairymen soon competed well with New York farmers in the Eastern markets and even in London. The "dairy revolution," however, would not be complete until the railroad network had spread over the entire state.

As a result of the Indian cessions of the 1830s and '40s, the United States government came into the possession of more than half the land in Wisconsin. Although some of the land was redistributed through auction sales with a minimum price of $1.25 an acre, Congress embarked upon a policy of using its landed wealth to encourage "internal improvements," such as railroad transportation. With one grant in 1856 and another in 1864 Congress turned over federal lands to the state of Wisconsin for the encouragement of railroad construction. The federal largesse amounted to about 10 percent of the total land area of the state. In 1870 the Chippewa *Herald* explained the rationale for giving public land to private companies for construction purposes:

What is the public domain good for while it remains public domain? We want cattle—not buffalo. We want sheep—not antelopes. We want emigrants—not Indians. Railroads will not be built through a howling wilderness without aid. Government loses nothing by the aid rendered. It is true, settlers pay more for land, but is there not a large amount of public domain for them to select from? ... I fear [referring to the opposition to land grants] *that the same spirit is alive that opposed free schools, free men, and free homesteads.*

The land grants may have hastened by several years the installation of a few miles of track, but most of the grants were wasted on promoters who secured patents and then lost all interest in construction. From beginning to end, the story of railroad land grants in Wisconsin is a dreary recital of extensions of time, forfeitures and reissued grants, all of which dissipated the energy and ultimately the moral authority of the Legislature.

In reality, small groups of investors with a limited goal, such as a desire to connect two cities, put down most of the railroad track laid in the 19th century. The major trunk lines of Wisconsin were created by consolidating the smaller, independent lines. The consolidation movement began with the old La Crosse & Milwaukee Railroad, which completed a line across the southern part of the state in the 1850s. After undergoing bankruptcy in 1863, it was reorganized as the Milwaukee & St. Paul Railway Company under the presidency of Scottish-born Alexander Mitchell, Wisconsin's version of New York's railroad empire builder, Cornelius Vanderbilt. Mitchell was also president of the Chicago & Milwaukee Railroad, and he simply merged the two lines. Through a stock market scam worthy of a Vanderbilt he acquired control of his chief competitor, the Milwaukee and Prairie du Chien, and by 1869 Mitchell controlled all the traffic between Lake Michigan and the Mississippi.

Reorganizing his company as the Chicago, Milwaukee, St. Paul & Pacific Railroad (or "Milwaukee Road") Mitchell was laying plans for expansion across Iowa when he looked over his shoulder and saw competition from the rapidly expanding Chicago & North Western Railroad. This corporation had begun as a small "feeder" line in the Rock River Valley, and through acquisitions it eventually connected Chicago, Rockford and Madison. It then moved into the newly opened pinelands in the Fox and Wolf river valleys. Undaunted, Mitchell hastened to bring the North Western into his web. When the president of the North Western died in 1869, Mitchell was chosen to fill his place. He was then in command of a railroad empire stretching from Chicago north to Lake Superior and west to Omaha. His 2,300 miles of track exceeded that of Vanderbilt's still uncompleted New York Central System, and for one heady moment Mitchell was the railroad king of the world.

Besides bringing Wisconsin into the national—even international—economy, the railroads had a huge impact on community development and the state's social life. The Wisconsin Central, one of the few lines in the state outside Mitchell's control, built communities of its own to serve. It originated with a land grant to build a line connecting Menasha on Lake Winnebago with Ashland on Lake Superior's Chequamegon Bay. In 1871 the promoters began construction at each end of the line. The first stretch, from Menasha to Stevens Point, was completed by the end of the year, but the real challenge lay in the remaining 187 miles of wilderness, lakes and highlands between Stevens Point and Ashland. The latter had a population of five when the railroad surveyors arrived.

A sudden influx of lumbermen, workers and innkeepers transformed Ashland into a boom town of 200 buildings by the end of 1872. The Colby family, which had made a fortune in textiles during the war and had invested much of their wealth in the railroad, built a sprawling 400-room wooden hotel, the Chequamegon. In short order the crew working south from Ashland constructed the first 30 miles to the Penokee Gap in the northern highlands, but then the project bogged down, defeated by the rugged terrain and a financial depression that struck the country in 1873. The link to Stevens Point was not completed until 1877. In the meantime, Ashland thrived. The Wisconsin Central discovered high-grade iron ore in the Penokee Hills in 1873, and the wharfs built in Ashland to bring in supplies to railroad workers were expanded to accommodate ore boats.

In the 1880s a consortium of Minneapolis promoters, using existing lines and new construction, built a railroad from Duluth east to the Sault Ste. Marie. The idea was to shortcut the water route across Lake Superior, which was closed by ice five months of the year. Through connections in Minneapolis with western railroads, the "Soo Line" could tap the entire northern plains. The immediate beneficiary was Superior, Wisconsin, which lay on a flat flood plain at the end of the lake, and was more convenient than Duluth to the route of the Soo Line along the south shore. James J. Hill, then in the process of building the Great Northern Railroad across the

Plains to the Pacific, constructed a grain-shipping terminal at Superior, with storage elevators and loading docks. When the Mesabi Iron Range in Minnesota began yielding high-quality iron ore in the 1890s, Hill built a complex of loading docks in Superior. Both Ashland and Superior prospered until after the turn of the century, but a harsh climate, exhaustion of the ore fields and the declining importance of their railroad connections prevented them from achieving the cosmopolitan importance to which they aspired.

By the 1880s the train whistle was part of the daily sounds that accompanied the rhythm of life for most Wisconsinites. The state had almost 4,000 miles of track in use by 1883 and almost 6,000 a decade later. In 1890, 30 scheduled trains arrived in Janesville every day, a level of service not unusual for a southern Wisconsin city. Telegraph lines were strung along the railroad rights of way because railroad managers used the lines to manage traffic and enforce safety rules. As a result, nearly every depot had a Western Union Telegraph office, providing instantaneous communication with the outside world. Adding to the information explosion was the daily arrival of metropolitan newspapers and national magazines. Mail-order catalogues brought the latest gadgetry and up-to-date fashions to the most remote of rural hamlets. The railroad also brought carnival troops, traveling salesmen, lecturers on the Chautauqua circuit and statewide political candidates—access, in short, to the whole wide world.

In addition to affecting the economy and the lifestyle of nearly every Wisconsin community, the railroads were at the center of the state's politics during the 1870s and '80s. Milwaukee Road president Alexander Mitchell had a commanding voice in the state Democratic Party and was a member of Congress from 1871 to 1875. The chief issue of the time was state railroad regulation, promulgated, not surprisingly, by farmers and urban shippers. Even after the brief union of the Milwaukee and North Western railroads under Mitchell's presidency was dissolved in 1870, the two railroads collaborated in setting freight rates. The result was that Wisconsin communities that were served by a single line paid higher freight rates than larger, but more distant, cities, such as St. Paul or Duluth, where other railroads provided competition. The Milwaukee Road derived two-thirds of its revenue from Wisconsin residents, though only half of its track lay inside the state.

Wisconsin farmers, acutely aware of this arithmetic, sought to protect their interests by forming local chapters of the national Society of Patrons of Husbandry, or "Grange." Although initially a social organization designed to relieve the isolation of rural life, the Grange inevitably turned to politics because the problems farmers faced, such as taxation and railroad regulation, could be solved only by political means. In 1873 the Grange joined with Democrats to overthrow the traditional Republican domination of the state government. Unfortunately, the Bourbon leaders of the Democratic Party, abetted by Alexander Mitchell, had no interest in railroad regulation. The election upset, however, was an alarm call to the Republicans, who sought to recover their traditional rural constituency by going after the railroads.

Wisconsin Central Railroad Terminus on Lake Superior at Ashland, ca. 1885.

The result was the Potter Law of 1874, a pioneering effort at government regulation of a private business. It set up a schedule of maximum rates for the railroads to charge (which was below those previously posted), and it set up a three-man commission to gather information on railroad economics and, if it seemed justified, to lower rates further. Typical of reform legislation in this period—an era that Mark Twain labeled the "Gilded Age"—the Potter Law was faulty in concept, poorly enforced, and sternly resisted by the railroads. Congressman Mitchell politely informed the Democratic governor that the law was unconstitutional and the Milwaukee Road would not abide by it. The North Western took the same position. The governor turned to the state Supreme Court and obtained a landmark opinion endorsing the right of the government to regulate a business that, although private in nature, served the public (anticipating a similar ruling by the United States Supreme Court in the case of Munn v. Illinois two years later). It was a hollow victory, for the railroads simply turned the screws, cutting services and halting construction. Neither Democrats nor Republicans had the stomach for a fight over government regulation, and the Potter Law was quietly repealed two years later.

▼

Politics and Community

The Gilded Age lives in infamy in the story of American politics, both for the corruption that permeated both federal and state governments and for the sterility of the political system. The fate of the Potter Law indicates that Wisconsin shared in the prevailing climate of political conservatism. Even local communities—those closest to, and presumably most responsive to, the electorate—were laggard in their responsibilities. The federal census of 1880 cited Beloit in a special volume of social statistics on cities. The city had no water system and no method of disposing of storm runoff or even of sewage—a condition it shared, incidentally, with larger cities such as Madison and Oshkosh. No ordinance governed the disposal of human waste, leaving it to the discretion of local householders. Householders commonly kept a cow to supply the family with milk and butter, and the animals roamed the streets nibbling on weeds and brush. A street crew occasionally gathered up the manure, spreading it on the unimproved public park. Madison did not banish cows until 1886, though a city ordinance 13 years earlier prevented them from grazing at will. The "cow question" occupied the city council of Janesville throughout the 1870s.

Though sluggish in developing sewage disposal, Oshkosh stood out among Wisconsin cities for its atmosphere of civic improvement, engendered by merchants' associations that thought public services and amenities would attract investment capital. Its downtown streets and stores were illuminated by electricity as early as 1882, only three years after Thomas A. Edison installed the first citywide electrical system in Menlo Park, New Jersey. Waterworks were being discussed, and a $30,000 opera house was under construction. The city had also landed a state normal school for the training of teachers, and it had wrested from rivals the site for the Northern State Insane Asylum.

By way of contrast, Mazomanie, on the western edge of Dane County, may have been more typical of Wisconsin's smaller communities. Founded as a bunkhouse settlement for Irish railroad workers—the remnants of which established a Catholic Church—the community soon attracted German immigrants. Although the town was overwhelmingly Republican, ethnic and religious divisions moved its politics. The merchants of main street dominated the village board, and when electricity reached the town in the mid-1880s, the board, with no sign of embarrassment, put the street lights in front of their own or their supporters' establishments. Sidewalks, the subject of many a meeting, were also strategically allocated. Only an embarrassed afterthought extended one to the "German church." The principal source of revenue for the village was the licensing of saloons, which may account for the generous allocation of funds for sidewalks, street improvements and lighting, to the neglect of other civic improvements.

The small towns of Wisconsin were nonetheless pleasant places in which to live and grow up. A young boy or girl could know everyone in town, enjoy the local festivals and visiting carnivals, and yet wander the meadows of the surrounding countryside. Speaking of Appleton, the town in which she grew up and began her writing career, Edna Ferber wrote in her *Autobiography*: "Creed, color, race, money—these mattered less in this civilized prosperous community than in any town I've ever encountered."

Such an environment was quite capable of producing greatness. Frederick Jackson Turner's father—named after President Andrew

Jackson—was a New England farmer who married an Adams County schoolteacher and settled in Portage as the owner and editor of the village's weekly newspaper. Portage in 1861, the year in which the future historian was born, had a population of 2,879, and 20 years later when Fred Turner graduated from the university at Madison it had grown to only 4,346. When he entered the university in 1878 Fred Turner was classed as a subfreshman because of the inadequacy of the Portage high school, even though he had taken a course in Greek in order to meet the university's classics requirement. The university, founded in the year of statehood and endowed by federal land grants during the Civil War, was beginning to get national recognition by the time Turner entered. Under John Bascom, who occupied the presidency from 1874 to 1887, its College of Agriculture became world-renowned and its liberal arts curriculum expanded beyond the classics to better meet the needs of the state's practical-minded citizenry. In Frederick Jackson Turner, village nurture and collegiate cosmopolitanism combined to produce one of the most influential scholars of the 20th century.

American politics in the 1870s and '80s was dominated by party bosses who thrived on the spoils of office. Each boss headed a machine that was lubricated by patronage. The chairman of the Wisconsin Republican Party through the 1870s, for instance, was the Madison postmaster with numerous federal jobs at his disposal. The dominant figure in the Wisconsin Republican Party in the following decade was Philetus Sawyer of Oshkosh, a millionaire lumberman who had served in Congress from 1865 to 1875, where he had gained a formidable knowledge of the national political labyrinth. He spent the next few years courting allies with an eye on the United States Senate. As he explained to his former colleague Cadwallader Washburn, "I have kissed a-s enough for the privlage of doing peoples Chores and I have got *through*." In 1881 the Legislature rewarded him with a seat in the Senate.

The Senate was the centerpiece of the United States government. The presidency had been weakened by the tribulations of Andrew Johnson and the scandals of Ulysses S. Grant. In addition, the rule of "senatorial courtesy" gave each senator a veto over presidential appointments in his state. This translated into a vast patronage apparatus, as each senator controlled the treasury and post office appointments within his domain. The patronage fueled his party machine and enabled him to control the Legislature, which obligingly kept him in his senatorial post. Less authoritarian than many of his colleagues, Sawyer moved gracefully through the corridors of power in Washington, while managing the Wisconsin Republican Party with tact and skill.

One of Sawyer's early recruits was John C. Spooner, a lawyer from Hudson who had an interest in the "Omaha Line," a mostly paper railroad that held various land grants in the northwestern part of the state. Spooner attached himself to Sawyer's banner when he spent the summer of 1880 stumping for legislative candidates who would support Sawyer's drive for a Senate seat. A flamboyant speaker, Spooner used the courtroom to win political influence. He confided to a political ally that his strategy was to accept cases for trial only in scattered locations in neighboring counties, where he could politick without being too obvious about it. With Sawyer's help Spooner was elected to the Senate in 1885 where he quickly joined the inner core of Republican leadership.

Another Sawyer ally was Jeremiah Rusk, who held the gover-

Life in a small town: the circus parade down Main Street.

nor's seat for three consecutive terms (1882-89), the longest tenure to that point in time. A successful Vernon County farmer, tavern keeper and stage owner near Viroqua, Rusk's huge form and patriarchal beard made an imposing political figure. He was a popular governor essentially because his own interests were in accord with those of a large part of the electorate. A successful farmer, he took an interest in the university's department of agriculture and was a strong ally of William A. Henry, who became dean of the newly created College of Agriculture in 1891.

Almost alone among political figures of the time, Rusk displayed some sympathy for the down and out. Chronic unemployment was one of the byproducts of industrialization and farm mechanization. People wandering the countryside seeking work were looked on with extreme disfavor, being described variously as "vagrants" or "vagabonds." Beginning in 1879 the Legislature regularly entertained measures designed to punish vagabonds and induce them to keep moving until they left the state. In 1883 Rusk allowed one such measure to become law without his signature, but when the Legislature tightened the screws on the poor a year later, Rusk acted. The 1884 amendment allowed counties to put vagrants in jail for up to 90 days on a diet of bread and water. In a ringing veto message Gov. Rusk pointed out that this punishment was more harsh than that imposed on hardened criminals placed in solitary confinement in Waupun. He characterized the legislation as sheer terrorism, and the message made good newspaper copy. Summarized a Milwaukee journalist: "No man in my time as a reporter, who occupied the exalted post of governor of the Badger State was more popular with the masses than Jeremiah Rusk, former stage driver."

Although Republicans controlled the state government from the beginning of the Civil War till 1890, the Democrats were not utterly helpless. They had strong popular support in the counties along Lake Michigan and among German Catholic and Irish voters. Their problem was a weak organization and the lack of any ideas that might have distinguished them from the Republicans. A conservative Bourbon element, symbolized by railroadman Alexander Mitchell, was in firm control of the party apparatus.

The election of Grover Cleveland in 1884—the first Democratic President since before the Civil War—put a spark of life into Wisconsin's Democratic Party, even though the state had gone for Cleveland's opponent, James G. Blaine. Cleveland appointed William F. Vilas postmaster general of the United States. A Madison attorney and a member of the university board of regents, Vilas had been the acknowledged leader of the Democratic Party since the mid-1870s. The federal post office, which controlled three-fourths of nonmilitary federal employees, was the chief patronage post in the nation. Village postmasters were of vital political importance because they were in a position to distribute party materials and provide advice on who was fit for political office. With post offices throughout the state (as well as the country) changing hands after 1885, senators Sawyer and Spooner were cut off from the patronage spigot, and Democrats enjoyed a rare moment of employment. The moment was all too brief, as President Cleveland fell to Republican Benjamin Harrison in 1888, but the Democrats would be back four years later, benefiting from a popular uprising occasioned by a Republican effort to "Americanize" education.

The controversy over the Bennett Law was the most serious political crisis of the time. It also foretold the end of the political complacency that had characterized the Gilded Age and the dawn of a new—more earnest—political climate.

Wisconsin had provided tax-supported public education since statehood, and it had required elementary schooling of all young people since 1879. Side by side with the public schools, however, was a strong parochial school system, financed and controlled by the German community. In this system German was the standard language. If students learned English at all, they did so by rote memory, as a foreign language, and acquired a tourist's capacity to handle grocery clerks and railroad conductors. Governor Rusk and his superintendent of education were not concerned about the equivalency of public and parochial education. To Rusk, literacy was literacy, whether in English or in German; schooling of any sort was the objective. Rusk also knew that parochial schools, a carryover from the old country, were as essential to the German community as the church and the German-speaking home.

Into this somnolent hornet's nest leaped William Dempster Hoard, elected governor in 1889 as a partial reward for his contributions to the state's dairy industry. Hoard brought to the post the perspective of a small-town journalist who was expected to have insights on a wide variety of topics. He thus viewed education—not unreasonably—as an introduction to the cultivated arts of mankind.

Bicyclists in Green Bay, ca. 1890. The "safety bicycle" with equally sized wheels was introduced in the 1880s. Cyclists, who took their sport seriously, joined farmers who wanted access to markets in promoting the "good roads movement" at the turn of the century.

That included a working knowledge of English, the gateway to American culture. As a result, in his opening message to the Legislature, he called for instruction in English in all schools of the state.

The result was the Bennett Law, named after an Iowa County Irish Catholic assemblyman who had little to do with its authorship. Drafters of the law initially intended to attack child labor by requiring schooling of every child between the ages of 7 and 14. However, they defined "school" in terms of curriculum, and the prescribed curriculum included reading, writing, arithmetic and United States history, all taught in the English language.

The regulation of parochial schools was at that time a contentious issue in Bismarck's Germany. Sensing that Wisconsin was on a similar secular track, the German Lutherans allied with the Catholic hierarchy—which commanded allegiance among both Germans and the growing Polish minority—and created a furor unknown since the Civil War. Democrats, who had not been committed to education or any other social issue, found a sudden currency in their neutrality. The result was a political revolution in 1890 that swept Democrats into control of both the governorship and the Assembly. Senator Spooner, understandably bitter because his term expired in March 1891, said of the debacle: "The school law did it—a silly, sentimental, and damned useless abstraction, foisted upon us by a self-righteous demagogue." Predictably, the Democratic Assembly repealed the Bennett Law in 1891 and sent William F. Vilas to the U.S. Senate. The momentum continued into 1892 when the Democrats added to their strength in the Assembly, re-elected their governor, and gave the state's electoral vote to a Democratic presidential candidate, Grover Cleveland, for the first time in 40 years.

The financial panic of 1893 and the ensuing depression—the worst of the century—demonstrated the inability of Bourbon Democrats, such as President Cleveland and his Wisconsin cohorts, to respond to the compelling needs of an urban-industrial society. Labor strife and the drain of gold from the federal treasury destroyed Cleveland's influence before he had been in office two years. Republicans returned to power, both in Congress and in the state of Wisconsin, in 1894. Yet the superficial rivalry between the two dominant political parties masked a growing dissatisfaction with the system itself. What the disaffected needed was a competent, pragmatic leader.

Among the casualties in the Republican debacle of 1890 was Congressman Robert M. La Follette. Farm-bred, La Follette had given up the rural life in favor of law school at the University of Wisconsin, subsequently opening a practice in Madison. To the end of his life La Follette contended that his political ideology was shaped by Edward G. Ryan, Irish-born lawyer from Racine and one of the founders of the state Democratic Party. In 1873 Ryan addressed the graduating class of the university, and La Follette, who was in the audience, never forgot the speech. With deep foreboding, Ryan warned his audience: "There is looming up a new and dark power. ... For the first time really in our politics money is taking the field as an organized power. Money as a political influence is essentially corrupt; by far the most dangerous to the free and just administration of the law. An aristocracy of money is essentially the coarsest and rudest, the most ignoble and demoralizing, of all aristocracies. ... It is entitled to fear, if not respect. The question will arise, and arise in your day, though perhaps not fully in mine, 'Which shall rule—wealth or man; which shall lead—money or intellect; who shall fill public stations—educated and free patriotic men, or the feudal serfs of corporate capital.' "

La Follette opened a successful law practice in Madison and, beginning in 1885, served three terms in the U.S. House of Representatives. In Congress he curried the favor of Speaker Thomas B. "Czar" Reed and adhered to the Republican Party line on such issues as the tariff (high rates to protect American industries) and railroad regulation (little or none). But after losing his seat in 1891 Edward G. Ryan's words came back to haunt him. The occasion was the so-called "Treasury Cases." For many years Wisconsin's state treasurers had deposited the state's monies in favored banks ("pet banks"). This was not illegal because neither law nor the state constitution specified what to do with the funds, and keeping them in a vault was impractical. The catch was that the banks paid interest on the money, but the interest was never credited to the state. It was a common assumption that the money was collected by political subordinates and spent for party purposes. As Republican party boss, Senator Sawyer had served as bondsman for many of the state treasurers, and he was probably the chief beneficiary of the scam. When the Democrats gained control of the state, the attorney general began an investigation, and the trail led directly to an Oshkosh bank of which Sawyer was a principal stockholder.

In the ensuing litigation Sawyer stood to lose as much as $200,000 as bondsman to the treasurers, and a great deal more in political capital and loss of reputation. As La Follette later told the story, Sawyer asked to meet with him at the Plankinton Hotel in

Milwaukee. Assuming that the meeting was to discuss political strategy, La Follette was dumbfounded when Sawyer opened the conversation with talk of the treasury cases. "These cases are awfully important to us," Sawyer continued. "I don't want to hire you as an attorney in the cases, and don't want you to go into court. But here is fifty dollars. I will give you five hundred more or a thousand ... when Siebecker decides the cases right." Robert Siebecker, the Dane County judge who would hear the cases, was La Follette's brother-in-law. The proffered bribe revealed the moral bankruptcy of the old political order, and La Follette stalked from the room while Sawyer was trying to rephrase the offer. In his autobiography the man who ushered in a new era in Wisconsin politics wrote: "Nothing else ever came into my life that exerted such a powerful influence upon me as that affair. ... Out of this awful ordeal came understanding, and out of understanding came resolution. I determined that the power of this corrupt influence, which was undermining and destroying every semblance of representative government in Wisconsin, should be broken."

▼

Travelers' Guide
Logging Era

Cook-Rutledge Mansion, 505 W. Grand Ave., Chippewa Falls; (715) 723-7181. Home of one of the city's prominent lumber barons.

Empire in Pine Lumber Museum, First Street, Downsville; (800) 283-1862, (715) 235-9087. Re-created blacksmith shop, cook shanty and other elements of a logging camp, along with photographs and a slide show.

Holt Balcolm Logging Camp, County F, Lakewood; (715) 276-7623. Restored bunkhouse and cook shanty.

Iron County Historical Museum, 303 Iron St., Hurley; (715) 561-2244. Memorabilia of the area's logging and farming heritage.

Lumberjack Special and Camp Five, Highway 8, Laona; (800) 774-3414. Steam-train rides, logging museum and forest tram tours.

Marathon County Historical Society, 403 McIndoe St., Wausau; (715) 848-6143. Victorian-period rooms and exhibits relating the region's lumbering history in the former home of lumber baron Cyrus Yawkey.

Marinette County Logging Museum, Highway 41, Marinette; (715) 732-0831. Photographs, artifacts and a diorama of a logging camp.

Menominee Logging Camp Museum, County VV, Keshena; (715) 799-3757. Large collection of logging artifacts.

Oshkosh Public Museum, 1331 Algoma Blvd., Oshkosh; (414) 424-4730. Exhibits on Oshkosh's logging era.

Paul Bunyon Logging Camp, Carson Park, Eau Claire; (715) 835-6200. Re-created 1890s logging camp with exhibits and films that depict the work of the lumbermen.

Peshtigo Fire Museum, 400 Oconto Avenue, Peshtigo; (715) 582-3244. Relates the story of the greatest fire disaster in United States history.

Polk County Museum, Main Street, Balsam Lake; (715) 485-9269. Exhibits include logging memorabilia.

Presque Isle Heritage Society Museum, Main Street, Presque Isle; (715) 686-2910. Artifacts and clothing from the area's logging days.

Rhinelander Logging Museum, Oneida Avenue, Rhinelander; (715) 369-5004. Reproduction of a logging camp, with antique logging equipment and narrow-gauge rail cars.

Rusk County Historical Museum, County Fairgrounds, Edgewood Avenue East, Ladysmith; (715) 532-3633. Exhibits depicting the area's logging industry.

St. Croix National Scenic Riverway, Massachusetts and Hamilton Streets, St. Croix Falls; (715) 483-3284. Visitors center contains exhibits on logging along the St. Croix River.

Washburn County Historical Museum, 200 W. Second Ave., Shell Lake; (715) 468-2982. Artifacts from the region's logging era.

Lumberjack World Championships, Highway B, Hayward; (715) 634-2484. Lumbermen compete in log rolling, chopping, sawing and tree-climbing contests; held the last weekend in July.

Agriculture

Antique Power, Steam and Threshing Show, intersection of Highways B and I, Burnett. Demonstrations of threshing, corn harvesting and baling on antique machinery; held the first weekend in August by the Dodge County Antique Power Club.

Heritage Hill State Park, 2640 S. Webster Ave., Green Bay; (414) 448-5150. Restored Belgian farm depicts agricultural life at the turn of the century.

Historic Cheesemaking Center, 1211 17th Ave., Monroe; (800) 307-7208. Replica of a 19th-century cheese factory and historic photographs.

Hoard Historical Museum and National Dairy Shrine, 407 Merchants Ave., Fort Atkinson; (414) 563-7769. Recounts the history of dairying in Wisconsin.

Sheboygan County Museum, 3110 Erie Ave., Sheboygan; (414) 458-1103. Restored 1867 cheese factory contains antique cheesemaking equipment and an exhibit on Wisconsin's cheese factories.

Railroading

Chippewa Valley Railroad, Carson Park, Eau Claire; (800) 344-FUNN. Train rides using a variety of equipment including coal-fired steam locomotives and wooden 1880s-style passenger coaches.

East Troy Electric Railroad Museum, 2002 Church St., East Troy; (414) 548-3837. Dedicated to the electric railways that connected outlying communities to Milwaukee.

Elroy-Sparta State Trail, Kendall Depot, Kendall;

(608) 463-7109. Bicycle trail on the former Chicago and North Western railroad bed goes through three tunnels built in 1873. Restored depot in Kendall contains historic railroad photos and artifacts.

Fennimore Railroad Historical Society Museum, 610 Lincoln Ave., Fennimore; (608) 822-6144. Exhibits on railroading, including the "Dinky" narrow-gauge train that operated in the area.

Mid-Continent Railway Museum, 8 E-8948 Diamond Hill Rd., North Freedom; (608) 522-4261. Steam-train rides depart from a historic depot.

National Railroad Museum, 2285 S. Broadway, Green Bay; (414) 437-7623. Eighty restored locomotives and rail cars, train rides and a slide show on the history of rail service.

Northern Wisconsin Interpretive Center, 400 Third Ave. West, Ashland; (715) 682-6600. Exhibits, housed in the historic Soo Line depot, describe the coming of the railroad to this important port.

Town Life

Milwaukee Public Museum, 800 W. Wells St., Milwaukee; (414) 278-2702. Re-created "Streets of Old Milwaukee" show the sights and sounds of the city near the turn of the century.

Stonefield Village, County VV, Cassville; (608) 725-5210. Replica of an 1890s village, operated by the State Historical Society, with costumed guides interpreting town life.

Chapter 6

THE LA FOLLETTE ERA

I t is tempting to point to the year 1901 as the beginning of the era of political and social reform known as the Progressive Movement. That was the year in which Theodore Roosevelt acceded to the presidency of the United States and Robert M. La Follette became governor of Wisconsin. In fact, both men were rather belated adherents to the cause of reform, the roots of which lay in the previous decade.

The basic thrust of Progressivism was to return power to "the people," that is, the consumers and taxpayers of the nation. The "ills of democracy," according to the Progressive diagnosis, stemmed from the fact that the political system had succumbed to "hidden government"—boss rule—and the bosses were sustained by contributions from great, impersonal corporations that needed political favors, notably the public utilities and the railroads. The main thrust of Progressive reform was to restore the average voter to his rightful place at the foundation of the political system, as he supposedly had been in the days of Jefferson, Jackson and Lincoln. The political reforms that they hoped would break the power of the establishment included the primary, which would give voters a voice in the nomination process, and popular election of U. S. Senators. They also advocated the initiative and referendum, which would give the people a role in legislation; women's suffrage; and corrupt practices acts that would eliminate bribery and curtail lobbyists. The Progressives' economic program included municipal ownership of utilities, government regulation of railroads, and income and inheritance taxes that would provide a more equitable distribution of wealth.

The reform movement cut across party lines and divided both Republicans and Democrats. The reformers themselves were divided, as evidenced by the wary competition between La Follette and Roosevelt for leadership of the Republican insurgents. The two men kept each other at arm's length and, in private, each expressed nothing but contempt for the other. Yet La Follette and Roosevelt were alike in one important respect. Each had a gift for oratory and a command of the rhetoric of protest. The legislative accomplishments of each were actually rather meager. Their contribution instead was to popularize the aims of the reformers and, by lending their own rhetorical support, to make Progressivism respectable. That was no mean accomplishment, for the reform efforts of earlier decades, led by farm and labor organizations, had foundered on the rock of public ridicule. The Populists of the 1880s and '90s had been dismissed by middle-class America as a collection of hayseeds and wild-eyed fanatics.

Progressivism was a middle-class, largely urban movement led by fundamentally conservative men such as La Follette, Roosevelt and, ultimately, Woodrow Wilson. Yet it built upon the anguished cries of bankrupt farmers and unemployed workers heard throughout the previous decade.

▼

Seeds of Protest

Religious and ethnic divisions governed American voting behavior in the period between the Civil War and 1900. The Republican Party had been born on the eve of the Civil War as a Northern institution, anti-slavery and anti-Catholic. For the remainder of the century in Wisconsin it attracted Protestants, whether transplanted Yankees, German Lutherans or Scandinavians, all of whom burned with moral indignation at the power of Southern slaveholders and the foreign Pope. As a result, German Catholics and the Irish drifted into the Democratic Party, whose main strength lay in the lake counties in the southeastern part of the state. Since the rest of the state was heavily Republican, the Republicans were normally in control. Election patterns confirmed the shrewd observation of a Grand Rapids editor that "the natural tendency is to sustain by your vote that party to which your father belonged—into which you originally drifted without consideration, and in which you have remained by force of association and habit."

Because prejudices ran deep, feelings ran high at election time, and voters turned out in huge numbers. Election day was a time of socializing, and the polling place had the atmosphere of a carnival. Politicians catered to the biases of the electorate in their speeches, but they made few promises, recognizing that religious and ethnic hatreds were best left unaddressed by the political system. As a result they went off to the legislative session in Madison without ideological commitment, and this made them subject to boss rule and corporate influence.

The Gilded Age tradition, in Wisconsin as in other states, was to send the most prominent man in the dominant party to the United States Senate. In Wisconsin this was Philetus Sawyer, who remained the acknowledged leader of the Republican Party even after losing his Senate seat to the Democrats in 1892. Yet in every state political organization there was also a behind-the-scenes boss, who often held a discreet, patronage-loaded job such as postmaster general. This was the man who managed day-to-day political activities and looked after the interests of corporate contributors. In Wisconsin this position was filled by Henry C. Payne, postmaster of Milwaukee from 1876 to 1885, postmaster general of the United States under President William McKinley from 1897 to 1901, and renamed postmaster of Milwaukee by Theodore Roosevelt in 1901, holding that position until his death.

Possessed of an unremarkable face partially hidden by a bushy mustache, Payne looked more like a village shopkeeper than a villain, yet he was the most hated man in the state by the mid-1890s. Temporarily bereft of political office while the Democrats governed in Washington in the mid-1880s, Payne had turned his organizing talents to business management. He became president of the fledgling Wisconsin Telephone Company in 1889, and in subsequent years he was named to the board of directors of several corporations, including the Milwaukee Railroad. In 1890 a syndicate of Eastern capitalists hired him to consolidate Milwaukee's electric streetcar lines and lighting companies into a single monopoly. Known as a "sweet singer" before legislative committees, Payne obtained enough preferments, franchises and tax breaks for his company to give it control of all the electric power and public transportation in the state's largest city. In this dominant position he reaped a rich harvest in financial profits and public loathing.

Wisconsin politics during the 1880s and early 1890s thus presented a rather placid scene of gentlemanly competition for the spoils of office. There were nevertheless undercurrents of protest that gradually discredited the system of boss rule. Prime among these was the crusade against vice—just the sort of social reform that the political leaders would have preferred to ignore. Crusades against the saloon and the prostitute and in favor of the observance of the Sabbath were deeply rooted in Wisconsin's ethnic and religious traditions, but they were also a lingering echo of pre-Civil War reform fervor. Just as slavery was the engrossing evil of antebellum America, intemperance seemed to be the great sin of the Gilded Age. "Since the abolition of chattel slavery," declared a convention of Wisconsin Congregationalists in 1880, "the providence of God seems to be pressing the temperance reform to the front, as the next great question to be passed upon by the American people."

The Legislature periodically yielded to the pressure from the churches. In 1849 it enacted the first Sunday law, banning sports and amusements on God's day of rest. In 1861 the reformers secured a law banning the sale of liquor near churches, schools and public institutions. In 1874 the Legislature allowed cities and towns to regulate the license fees of saloons, and four years later it banned the sale of liquor on Sundays. The vice laws allowed the legislators to clear their consciences, while leaving enforcement up to others. And enforcement depended on local pressure. The problem, as the leading humorist of the day, Finley Peter Dunne, pointed out, was that crusaders were only good "f'r a short distance" and the crusade collapsed after "th' first sprint." People get tired of rectitude and "want somewhere to go nights," and one day the "boss crusader finds that he's alone in Sodom."

Frustrated, the vice crusaders turned their spears on the politicians. The world of politics, said one religious journal, was "like a barroom in the possession of hard characters," and saloonkeepers were "protected rather than exterminated by the 'strong arm of the civil law.'" To raise the moral level of Wisconsin politics, crusaders entered local elections, seeking to elect candidates who would enforce the vice laws. They made little progress, but their trenchant critique of the system helped to discredit the Old Guard.

One of the signal accomplishments of the vice crusade was to bring women into the public arena. The prevailing view in the Victorian era was that a woman's place was in the home, but society tolerated public appearances in defense of the home and family. Because the consumption of alcohol threatened the family and wasted its resources, women commanded attention when they took the public stage and denounced intemperance. The Women's Christian Temperance Union (WCTU), formed in the early 1870s, was the largest and best organized of the vice crusades. The war against the saloon, in turn, resurrected the women's suffrage movement that had been born before the Civil War. Frances Willard, who grew up on a farm near Janesville and served as president of the WCTU until her death in 1898, recognized that to be effective in the cause of temperance women must obtain the ballot. The Women's Suffrage Association took an even broader view, predicting "an improvement of social conditions in direct proportion to the increase of woman's influence." The two movements reinforced one another. In 1888, for instance, all 80 members of the WCTU in Marathon County were suffragettes.

Like other vice crusaders, the feminists became critical of the political establishment. Their chief opponents were recent arrivals from Germany and Ireland, poverty-stricken and unlettered men who enjoyed their beer on Sunday and had little use for politically minded females. Suffragettes surmised that the city and state political machines rested on the votes of these untutored and immoral males, and no social reform was possible until there was political reform. Suffragettes and vice crusaders alike were thus prepared to make an instant hero of anyone who challenged the party bosses.

The Old Guard probably would have survived these assaults had Wisconsin—and the nation—continued to prosper economically. But in 1893 a financial panic ushered in five years of depression, the most severe by far of the 19th century. Banks failed, businesses went bankrupt, and factories were shut down. Unemployment became a serious national problem for the first time in American history. Even the middle class felt the pinch of poverty, and everywhere people looked for something or someone to blame. "On every corner," declared the *Superior Evening Telegram*, "stands a man whose fortune in these dull times has made him an ugly critic of everything and everybody."

In an age of steady economic growth it had been possible to believe that certain persons were poor because of some character flaw, a lack of industry or thrift. But in hard times, when a third of a community was unemployed and 20 percent wage cuts were driving men to strike, poverty could not be dismissed. It was a product of the system itself, a flaw in the national fabric.

The depression also called attention to the growing gap between rich and poor. Millionaires like Philetus Sawyer and Henry C. Payne seemed little affected by the depression, even though some of their paper wealth might have evaporated. One journalist declared: "Men are rightly feeling that a social order like the present, with its enormous wealth side by side with appalling poverty, its luxury for a few and its pre-mortem hell for many, with its war between labor and capital, cannot be the final form of human society." The Milwaukee women's club, previously given to discussions of literature, devoted its 1895-96 winter session to the topic of "The Idle Rich and the Idle Poor." With America looking more and more like decadent, class-ridden Europe, democracy itself seemed to be at stake.

Some thought the free enterprise system ought to be scrapped altogether. The ideas of Karl Marx—popularly known at the time as the "German philosophy"—had filtered into the United States following the 1870 French uprising that had resulted in the formation of the first Communist Internationale. Marx's theories found considerable support among working-class Germans of Milwaukee, but his predicate of a "proletarian revolution" was unacceptable to most Wisconsinites, as well as other Americans. Victor Berger, an Austrian Jew by birth, gave socialism an American cast by rejecting the idea of class revolution and advocating gradual change through piecemeal reforms. His Social Democrat Party fielded a full ticket for municipal elections in 1898, and it was a force to be reckoned with in Milwaukee politics for two decades. Berger himself eventually represented the city and its environs in the United States Congress.

A less radical alternative was the "new economics" advocated by scholars such as Richard T. Ely. Trained in Germany, Ely gave up a professorship at prestigious Johns Hopkins University in order to join the faculty of the University of Wisconsin, attracted to the shores of Lake Mendota by the university's growing reputation for innovative scholarship. Ely rejected the classical notion that economics was a "pure" science governed by eternal verities, such as the "iron law of wages" (a Malthusian concept that overpopulation necessarily drove wages down to a level of bare subsistence). Peering at his seminars through round, steel-rimmed glasses, Ely taught that economics was an inductive science, subject to experiment. He thought government had an ethical role to play, in setting rules for fair competition, for instance, and encouraging labor organizations that would guard the welfare of workers. In 1894 Ely became the center of a controversy over academic freedom when a member of the university's board of regents denounced him as a radical. *The Nation*, a national news magazine, took up the charge. The board of regents conducted a public hearing that amounted to a "trial" of Ely's beliefs. In the end, the regents exonerated Ely and endorsed the principle of academic freedom. They resolved: "Whatever may be the limitations which trammel inquiry elsewhere we believe the great State University of Wisconsin should ever encourage that continual and fearless sifting and winnowing by which alone the truth can be found." Most of the state's newspapers supported Ely on grounds that the search for new economic prescriptions was so important that all ideas, no matter how radical, should be considered. The superintendent of schools in Madison went even farther. He thought the schools ought to reject "formalism" and tradition altogether, contending that only those teachers "who are thoroughly imbued with the progressive spirit of the times should be allowed to remain."

In 1896 the Fond du Lac school superintendent declared: "There was never a time when citizenship means as much as it does today. Public opinion ... is rapidly becoming more potent than the will of princes, and, what is more significant, every member of the body politic has a share in making this opinion." From the yeasty ferment of the depression arose a new civic consciousness, a dawning concept that there existed a "public interest" capable of solving common problems and resisting common enemies. Proclaimed an Appleton editor: "No man, however wealthy, can be independent of public opinion in matters appertaining to the public interest." This was the beacon that guided the La Follette insurgency.

▼

La Follette's Rise To Power

After losing his congressional seat in the Democratic landslide of 1890, La Follette returned to the practice of law, and his oratorical skills soon earned him a reputation as the foremost trial lawyer in the state. After he won damages for a client who had lost a hand in an industrial accident, the corporation's attorney angrily charged that La Follette "could not have made humanity's case any more desperate if it had been the hand of Providence that was lost." At the same time, La Follette never really left politics, seldom missing a chance to address a political picnic or camp meeting. In contrast to machine politicians like Sawyer and Payne, who avoided the masses, La Follette loved crowds. Insisting that everyone call him "Bob" (rare in a day when men preferred titles like "Colonel" or "Judge"), he had an unaffected, glad-handing sociability. By the mid-1890s he had adopted the rhetoric of insurgency, freely denouncing party bosses and political machines. Yet he remained in his own mind a loyal Republican. Instead of leaving the party, he planned to reshape it to his own ends. In 1896 he sought the Republican nomination for governor, but he lost when the party convention instead nominated the machine's candidate. Twenty delegates confessed to La Follette that they had been bribed by Sawyer's friends. Although La Follette loyally campaigned for the GOP ticket that fall, helping to carry Wisconsin for William McKinley, he brooded over his defeat at the hands of the party bosses.

La Follette's wife, Belle Case, in all likelihood abetted his conversion to the cause of reform. Of prominent Baraboo family (she retained her maiden name throughout her life), Belle Case was intensely ambitious and politically liberal. She was a graduate of the University of Wisconsin Law School, a rare achievement for a woman at that time. The pair had become engaged while at the university, but they were not married until 1881 for lack of money. Al-

Robert M. La Follette addressing a crowd from a farm wagon, Cumberland, 1897.

though she never practiced law, she was a shrewd political analyst and source of inspiration to La Follette, who commonly referred to her as "the Counselor." By the mid-1890s Belle was actively involved in the women's suffrage movement; she would later become an advocate of civil rights for blacks. The novelist Zona Gale once wrote of Mrs. La Follette that she ranked with Jane Addams and Lilian Wald (leaders of settlement houses in Chicago and New York) as "women of social passion" who used politics to "change the bitter conditions under which the majority of the human race support life." Her husband's politics were almost certainly colored by her thoughts and feelings.

In 1897 La Follette publicly broke with the Old Guard and announced his own program of Progressive reform. It had two elements—taxes on quasi-public corporations, such as railroads and utilities, and institution of a direct primary. The primary would allow voters a say in party nominations and undermine the power of machines. It would also work to the benefit of spellbinders like La Follette himself. The issues that La Follette chose had already met the test of popularity. Insurgent mayors had been elected in Milwaukee, Janesville, Ashland and Superior on promises to locate tax-dodgers and regulate the corporations.

Over the next three years La Follette built an organization of his own within the Republican Party. His technique was a blend of the old politics and the new. He courted politicians who had been squeezed out by the machine, like ex-governor William D. Hoard, and he appealed to the Scandinavian electorate, which had been taken for granted and ignored by Sawyer and Payne. But he also utilized the techniques of mass appeal pioneered by the urban reformers. After championing the direct primary in a speech at the University of Chicago and receiving favorable reports in the Chicago press, La Follette borrowed money from Hoard and printed 400,000 copies of the speech. In ensuing weeks more than 300 Wisconsin editors folded this free supplement into their papers.

By 1900 the once-formidable Republican machine was in a shambles. Sawyer died in March of that year, and reformers were in the saddle in Payne's Milwaukee. Payne was reduced to bribing a third of the city's aldermen in order to save his streetcar and lighting monopoly and had few friends, even among Republicans. The remnants of the conservative wing waited upon La Follette and received conciliatory treatment. With no fight at all he became the Republican nominee for governor. Although the Democratic nominee offered no real threat, La Follette campaigned with characteristic energy. He initiated the state's first whistle-stop campaign, traveling more than 6,000 miles and delivering 208 speeches in 61 counties. Although in popular vote he trailed McKinley, who was running once more against the hapless William Jennings Bryan, La Follette won 60 percent of the electorate and carried every county except a half-dozen Democratic bastions along the shore of Lake Michigan.

There was much to attract the new governor's attention as cries for change echoed across the state in 1901. Progressives in Milwaukee were still fighting Henry Payne's lighting and streetcar monopoly. Ashland was battling a private water company whose output was so impure that a typhoid epidemic had produced 500 cases of the disease and 30 deaths. Urban Progressives wanted to reign in the utilities by requiring popular referendums on the granting of franchises and by allowing cities to acquire their debts for public ownership. But La Follette refused to lend a hand to the cause of public utility reform. He instead gave single-minded attention to two issues on which he had been elected. Clearly, he did not want to dissipate his energies. Concern-

Belle Case La Follette addressing farmers, about 1915.

ing his decision to focus initially on railroad taxation, he wrote in his autobiography: "If we now attacked the larger problem of railroad regulation, as [many supporters] urged us to do, we should have too many issues to present clearly and thoroughly to the people in one campaign and would arouse the doubly bitter opposition of the railroads." He was sure that other reforms would follow in due course when the direct primary infused new blood into the political system.

His reforms were stalled by a Legislature dominated by Stalwarts (a term borrowed from Gilded Age politics that conservatives were beginning to use in referring to themselves), but he eventually secured them in 1902. After obtaining re-election in that year with the help of Democratic Progressives, he moved in a new direction, asking the Legislature for state regulation of railroad freight rates. The railroads, joined by the grain merchants and other large-bulk shippers who benefited from the existing rate structure, managed to defeat a bill setting up a regulatory commission. But that only gave La Follette a new issue on which to campaign in 1904.

In 1904 La Follette invented a new form of insurgent campaigning. He gathered together the roll-call votes of his opponents and toured the state in an automobile. (Automobiles had appeared in Wisconsin by 1900, and in 1905, when the state began requiring licenses, there were 1,492.) Invading the home districts of the Stalwarts, La Follette stood in his vehicle to explain to the curious assemblage at each crossroads the need for railroad regulation. He would then ask his audience to "look at the record," referring to his opponent's voting record. The implication was that the community's representative was a tool of the railroads. The contest, La Follette insisted, was a struggle between "government of the people" and government by public-service corporations. "Around that vital issue," he predicted, "the great political battles of the next twenty-five years will be fought out."

La Follette was also gaining national attention. When the Republican Party met in Chicago to nominate Theodore Roosevelt for a second term (his first had been a matter of filling out the term of assassinated William McKinley), the National Committee voted to seat the "federal" delegation, led by Senator Spooner, as the official one from Wisconsin. This action, cried La Follette, "has made the Wisconsin fight a national issue." He asked Republican voters "to rid the Republican Party of corporation control and again make it the party that it was in the days of Lincoln." The party went on to nominate Roosevelt, who defeated a characteristically feckless Democratic candidate. La Follette took no pleasure in Roosevelt's victory, regarding him as too much the errand-boy of party Stalwarts.

He did win a third term as governor, however, and he boasted that his "look at the record" technique had "cleaned up the Legislature." That was overstatement, for the railroads still had powerful friends in the state government. The Legislature did pass a rate regulation bill in 1905, but it contained numerous compromises. The railroad commission it created had no rate-fixing power; instead its powers were confined to investigation and review. And any decision it might make was subject to overturn by the courts. La Follette's rhetoric had placed Wisconsin on the map as the vanguard of Progressivism, but the railroad commission measure that he finally approved was in fact much weaker than that of several other states.

La Follette's disposition to compromise may have been due to an ambition for national office. The term of one of Wisconsin's United States senators expired in 1905, and Republican control of the Legislature assured La Follette a victory if he desired the seat. He agreed to serve on condition that he could retain the governorship until he saw his railroad commission bill through the Legislature. That accomplished, in 1906 he and Belle headed for Washington, D.C., and a new political stage.

▼

Wisconsin Reforms

While La Follette was in Washington the Progressive impulse in Wisconsin maintained a momentum of its own. A central feature of what became known as the "Wisconsin idea" was the use of highly trained experts in drafting laws and in staffing the regulatory commissions. Many of these were drafted from the campus of the University of Wisconsin. Charles R. Van Hise, a geologist by profession, became president of the university in 1903, and in his inaugural address he advocated that state agencies make more extensive use of the university and its scholarship. Gov. La Follette, who had been a classmate of Van Hise at the university, readily agreed. He instituted a Saturday Lunch Club to bring together state officials, legislators and members of the faculty with common interests.

Within a few years delegations arrived in Madison from all over the country to see firsthand how the university was serving the state. After returning home, the leader of an Arkansas delegation reported to Van Hise, "I am sure that the visit will be of great benefit to education in Arkansas. ... The University of Wisconsin is at the top and we are looking to you for counsel."

The most important of the scholar-administrators was John R. Commons, who was attracted to the university by Richard T. Ely in 1904. Commons had earned his Ph.D. at Johns Hopkins under the guidance of Ely, who had called his attention to the labor organizations of Baltimore. Commons became one of the first (and remains today one of the foremost) scholars to study the history of organized labor. He bounced through several teaching jobs before landing a distinguished chair at Syracuse University. However, the regents of that school found his economic theories far too progressive, and they abolished the chair in order to get rid of him. In his autobiog-

Charles R. McCarthy and the staff of the Legislative Reference Library, August 8, 1906.

raphy Commons described himself as "born again" when he arrived in Madison. Gov. La Follette, who had met Commons two years earlier, promptly put him to work drafting the state's first civil service law, which the Legislature approved in 1905.

The catalyst for the interaction between scholarship and legislation was the state's Legislative Reference Library, the singlehanded creation of a New England emigre of Irish descent, Charles McCarthy. After graduating from Brown University, McCarthy came to Madison to do graduate work in history under Frederick Jackson Turner. When the Legislature authorized a small appropriation for a "documents clerk" in 1901, Turner recommended McCarthy for the job. With consummate bureaucratic skill, McCarthy steadily enlarged his documentary holdings, his staff and his influence. In his autobiography John R. Commons explained how McCarthy's "bill factory" worked. Senator La Follette and the speaker of the state assembly had asked Commons to prepare a bill for the regulation of public utilities on the model of railroad regulation. "McCarthy gave me a room in his library, and during the five or six months' session of the Legislature I met there the representatives of the public utility corporations, and worked with Mr. M.S. Dudgeon, of McCarthy's legal staff, in drafting the bill." Commons added: "I did not, of my own initiative, introduce anything new in drafting the bill. I got it all from others. I was a kind of sieve for funneling ideas from everywhere into legislative enactment."

McCarthy added another feature to the "Wisconsin idea" (the phrase was the title of a book he wrote in 1912)—carrying the university to the people through an extension system. For some years the university had sporadically sent lecturers into the countryside; McCarthy's idea was to establish centers that could offer short courses in the liberal arts and agricultural sciences. He administered it through a department of his Legislative Reference Library and wheedled steadily increasing funding allotments from the Legislature. By 1912 the extension system had 63 branches around the state, including centers with permanent staffs at Milwaukee, La Crosse and Oshkosh.

Wisconsin's brand of Progressivism reached full flower during the administration of Francis E. McGovern, elected governor in 1910 and re-elected in 1912. McGovern received his political baptism in Milwaukee's struggle with the electric utility monopoly in the 1890s. His views were shaped by Victor Berger's socialists on one side and Milwaukee's German- and Irish-dominated Democratic Party on the other. La Follette regarded McGovern as a bit too radical, but he joined forces in 1910 because he needed McGovern's strength in the lakeshore counties for his own senato-rial re-election campaign. By 1910 the spirit of reform had so captured the popular imagination that even Stalwarts were describing themselves as Progressives. McGovern, who could also count on the votes of Berger's pragmatic socialists, thus faced a cooperative Legislature.

The first item on the agenda was workers' compensation. Injuries on the job had multiplied as factories became larger and more complex. Yet an injured worker could obtain compensation only by suing his employer and proving negligence. For some years labor unions in Wisconsin and elsewhere had demanded a state-mandated insurance fund for compensation without regard to fault. In 1911 John R. Commons undertook the job of drafting the legislation and winning political support. Though sympathetic to labor himself, Commons was able to enlist the support of all interests involved, manufacturers as well as labor unions. Farmers and village shopkeepers threw their support to the law when Commons exonerated businesses that employed fewer than four persons. The statute slipped noiselessly through the Legislature and became a model for other states.

The Wisconsin Industrial Commission was another of Professor Commons' offsprings. The statute establishing the commission gave it broad powers and ample discretion. Its advisory committees, consisting of representatives of management, labor and the public, all guided by experts, were to establish codes for "reasonable conditions" of safety in each industry. Since the courts' interpretation of the term "reasonable" in prior statutes had deprived it of any meaning, Commons and McCarthy wrote a definition into the statute. They defined it as "the highest degree of safety, health and well-being of the employees that the nature of the industry or employment would reasonably permit." With that, "reasonable" meant "state of the art" precautions as defined by the experts. Commons himself served as the resident expert on the commission for its first five years.

The "Wisconsin idea," mature by 1912, was adopted in whole or in part by many other states. McCarthy's description of it, published in that year, no doubt helped to spread the gospel. Yet, just as the Progressive spirit reached its apex nationally in 1912 with the election of Woodrow Wilson, it ran out of gas in Wisconsin. The fault was largely La Follette's.

▼

Progressivism Declines

In the Senate La Follette had joined Progressives of both parties to obtain federal regulation of railroads in 1906, though he was disgusted with President Roosevelt for accepting what Roosevelt himself admitted was "half a loaf." The concessions Roosevelt agreed to were almost exactly those that La Follette had accepted in Wisconsin. La Follette had his eye on the Republican nomination when Roosevelt retired, and he was disappointed when the party turned instead to Roosevelt's choice, William Howard Taft. Taft won election in 1908 on a promise to lower the tariff, which Progressives claimed protected domestic monopolies from foreign competition. He then agreed to a compromise measure that actually left the rates unchanged.

That fiasco handed the tariff issue to the Democrats, along with the closely related issue of big business and "trust busting." They campaigned in the off-year election of 1910 for lower prices on behalf of "the American housewife" (without offering to give her the vote) and won control of both houses of Congress. Democrats would control Congress for the next eight years. Taft was utterly discredited among Progressive Republicans, and La Follette revived his presidential ambitions. Unfortunately, so did Theodore Roosevelt. The ex-president returned from a hunting safari in Africa in 1910, disavowed Taft, and offered his own variety of Progressivism, which he labeled the "New Nationalism." Roosevelt's idea, essentially, was to make the president the "steward" of the people, using the power of the federal government to control big business and referee the game of free competition.

Regarding the New Nationalism as a reincarnation of Roosevelt's "half a loaf" philosophy, La Follette rejected the pleas of many Progressives that he join forces with the ex-President. In 1911 he formed the National Progressive Republican League with the aim of capturing control of the party's nominating convention in 1912 or, in the alternative, mounting a third-party insurgency. He failed in both. The party regulars renominated Taft; the Progressives bolted, formed a third party, and nominated Roosevelt. The Democratic candidate, Woodrow Wilson, won the three-way election, and with that the torch of Progressive leadership passed to the Democrats.

In Wisconsin, Gov. McGovern, like most Progressive Republicans, backed Theodore Roosevelt's candidacy in 1912, and La Follette could not forgive the personal slight. In McGovern's second term the La Follette men in the Legislature mounted a captious opposition to everything McGovern or his supporters proposed, and the state drifted for two years. In the mood of a "plague on both your houses," the voters sent a Stalwart Republican to the governor's mansion in 1914. The new resident had the good sense to retain the La Follette/McGovern reforms, but the spirit of innovation was gone. La Follette remained in the Senate, a lonely insurgent, unable to cooperate fully with either Republican or Democratic Progressives. He would achieve some victories, such as a 1916 law that regulated the hours of seamen involved in dangerous work (a pioneering piece of federal labor legislation), but he had lost his popular appeal.

By 1914 Progressivism was also on the wane nationally as the Wilson administration became increasingly preoccupied with foreign affairs. In his first two years in office President Wilson had accomplished momentous changes in the political economy of the nation—banking reform with the Federal Reserve Act, a strengthening of the antitrust laws and the establishment of a Federal Trade Commission to enforce rules of fair competition. Senator La Follette led a band of Republican insurgents who supported, albeit not wholeheartedly, the Wilsonian program. But he broke with Wilson on foreign policy, and the split between the two revealed a fundamental cleavage within the Progressive mentality.

A crisis with Mexico was brewing when Wilson took office. A revolution in 1910 expelled a corrupt dictator who had catered to foreign investors. Fearing that their investments were threatened by the revolutionary government, American businessmen financed a counterrevolution, and years of civil war ensued. La Follette instantly sympathized with the Mexican reformers, likening their battle with his own struggle against corporate business. By 1916, when the Wilson administration intervened in Mexico with a Punitive Expedition, La Follette had developed an insurgent's critique that linked corporate exploitation at home and abroad. Corporate privileges, he argued, returned more profits than could be invested in America. Never satiated, American business invested in weak and undeveloped countries where they could reap even bigger returns. When a target country resisted exploitation, the American investors asked the government for protection. As a result, La Follette bitterly opposed American intervention in Mexico, and he joined other

Camp Randall on June 21, 1912. Still an Army camp on the eve of World War I.

insurgents in opposing United States protectorates in Haiti and the Dominican Republic.

La Follette reacted in the same way to Woodrow Wilson's steady march toward American intervention in World War I. He felt that the only Americans who had a stake in the outcome of the war in Eu-

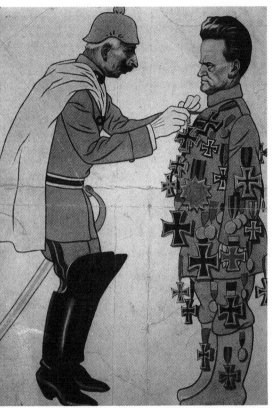

rope was the "War Trust"—bankers and munitions makers. La Follette conceded that the shipment of American food and munitions to the Allies gave a boost to the economy, with benefits to both farmers and factory workers, but he complained that it also brought inflation and hardship for consumers. When Wilson lent his support to the preparedness campaign in 1916, La Follette fumed that government munitions contracts were the ultimate robbery of taxpayers by privileged corporations. In April 1916 La Follette introduced a bill that would require an advisory referendum before the country could go to war. Wilson's Democratic majority blocked the measure, but, interestingly, the administration never denied La Follette's contention that a majority of Americans would have opposed entry into the war if given the opportunity to vote on it.

The Kaiser decorates La Follette for his vote against U.S. entry into World War I. Cover of newly founded Life *magazine in 1917.*

On April 2, 1917, President Wilson asked Congress for a declaration of war on Germany and the Central Powers, concluding that "the world must be made safe for democracy." In the ensuing debate

La Follette reminded the Senate that it was the poor, the Americans without power, who would be called upon to rot in the trenches, and he asked how one could have a war to save democracy without a popular vote on the question. A Southern senator retorted, somewhat irrelevantly, that La Follette was a better German than the German leaders. In the end, the Senate voted for war by 82 to 6, with two Republican Progressives and three Democrats joining La Follette in opposition. In the House of Representatives nine of Wisconsin's 11 members voted against the war. Nevertheless, it was La Follette's oratory that caught the nation's attention. Newspapers denounced the "traitor La Follette." Trumpeted one: "Henceforth he is the Man without a Country."

A sizable portion of Wisconsin's German population opposed American entry, but that did not hamper the state's contribution to the war effort. The state invested more than its share in the war bond drives, its factories converted swiftly to production of war material, and its farmers increased production with fewer laborers. The draft was carried on without obstruction, and the 32nd Division of the National Guard, made up of Wisconsin and Michigan men, had an outstanding combat record in the fields and trenches of France.

Wisconsin's congressional delegation opposed the war from idealism, not from any deference to their ethnic constituencies. And, in fearing that war would mean the end of reform, they were right, for Progressivism was the chief casualty of the conflict. With two exceptions: the temperance crusade and women's suffrage. Both of these movements, forerunners of Progressivism, achieved their goals during the war. Their victories were the last heartbeat of reform.

▼

Temperance and Suffrage

Prior to the war the temperance advocates had met stubborn resistance in Wisconsin. In Wisconsin, as elsewhere in the nation, the Anti-Saloon League found its chief support among evangelical Protestants who believed that moral sanctions enforced by the government were essential to a decent society. The foreign-born population of Wisconsin, whether Irish Catholic or German Lutheran, felt that such state intervention in their lives was a threat to their culture and traditions. Many Germans preserved memories of the old country by spending Sunday afternoons at a beer garden. Financing the resistance was the state's beer industry. Wisconsin was third nationally in the production of beer, and the industry was of major economic importance.

The war changed all that. The entire German community

Women working at the Nash Motor Company, Kenosha, during World War I.

fell under suspicion, as native-born Americans came to believe that the German clubs and societies—formed years before to preserve German culture and traditions—were taking their orders from Berlin. It was not true. The German-American Alliance, the leading organization in the state with 37,000 members, devoted much of its energy during the war to attacking prohibitionists, rather than American foreign policy. Nevertheless, the prevailing suspicion diminished German influence in the state.

During the war prohibition blended with patriotism. A Yale economist wrote to Edward A. Ross, professor of sociology at the University of Wisconsin and a leading Progressive, that the prohibition of liquor "would save enough grain alone to make a loaf of bread for each of eleven million fighting men." It would also allow military physicians "to reduce greatly those contagious diseases that are the most prevalent among both soldiers and sailors." The Wilson administration seemed to agree. The Selective Service Act of 1918 set up "dry zones" around every military installation and forbade the sale or gift of alcohol to members of the armed services. Wilson's secretary of war extended the "dry zones" to the American encampments in France, fencing out prostitutes as well as liquor peddlers. Tightening the screws, Wilson, by presidential proclamation, limited the alcoholic content of beer to 2.75 percent. In December 1917 Congress approved and transmitted to the states an amendment to the Constitution authorizing the federal government to prohibit the manufacture, sale or export of intoxicating liquors.

The fight in Wisconsin over ratification of the amendment was down and dirty. The Wisconsin Brewers' Association draped itself in the Stars and Stripes and ran an advertisement pointing out that "the United States government is today collecting from the liquor industry alone in internal revenue more than enough money to pay each year the interest charge on all three Liberty Loans." The Anti-Saloon League countered with appeals to the public hostility toward Germans, contending that the great Milwaukee brewers, Pabst, Schlitz, Blatz and Miller, were "the worst of all our German enemies." The league condemned "Schlitzville on the lake" for producing "Kaiser brew" that brought social disorder and inefficiency.

The 18th Amendment went into effect after 36 states ratified. Wisconsin fell in line as the 39th. Congress imposed nationwide prohibition with the Volstead Act in 1919. Wisconsin's governor, John J. Blaine, a La Follette ally elected in 1920, would have to set the standard for the state's reaction to the law. Blaine was not an ardent wet, but he did worry about the invasion of privacy in sumptuary legislation. The Volstead act was utterly ambiguous. It prohibited the manufacture and sale of alcoholic beverages, including beer, but not the consumption. This was an open invitation for free enterprise to fill a void—consumer demand brought about illegal supply. In 1921 the Wisconsin Legislature sought to clarify the rules. It allowed people to make their own wine and beer. Blaine was satisfied, noting that "there can be no invasion of the home or any spying on family life under the bill, and it provides simplified machinery for enforcement." Whether this worked is another story.

The spirit of reform that prevailed throughout the nation after 1900 revived the women's suffrage movement, just as it did the temperance crusade. Suffragists benefited from the Progressives' stress on political equality and social justice, and they profited by the attitude, common among both sexes, that women were more principled and moral than men and hence a potentially humanizing influence in the governance of the American people. Both the La Follette Progressives and the Socialists endorsed women's suffrage after 1900. The core of the opposition was the liquor lobby and the foreign-born, both of whom feared "social feminism," the historians' label for the supposedly liberal influence of women on politics.

From its inception before the Civil War, the suffrage movement had concentrated on the state legislatures, for it was the states that controlled voting conditions. (The 15th Amendment merely required that the states extend the vote to blacks.) This tactic worked for a time. As early as the 1860s Western territories such as Wyoming and Montana extended the right to vote and hold office to women in order to attract women to their male-dominated mining society. By the 1890s, however, only a few states in the underpopulated West had gone along with the idea, and the National Women's Suffrage Association was nearly moribund. The influence of Progressivism was not felt until 1910 when the state of Washington voted for women's suffrage. The following year California followed suit, after a campaign that featured billboards, electric signs and essay contests. Three more states extended the vote to women in 1912, and Illinois allowed them to participate in presidential elections in 1913.

Seeking to build on this momentum, state Sen. David G. James of Richland Center, whose wife Laura had kept the Wisconsin Women's Suffrage Association alive in the gloomy days of the 1880s and 1890s, introduced a bill to submit the suffrage question to popular referendum in the general election of 1912. Militant women, unhappy with the spiritless Women's Suffrage Association, formed the Political Equality League to push the referendum. Ada James, the senator's daughter, was elected president of the league. With active assistance from Belle Case La Follette, James carried the suffrage message into every corner of the state. They failed, as voters rejected the referendum by 227,024 to 135,545. The attempt nevertheless educated many voters, and it gave the women experience in political organization.

In 1915 Carrie Chapman Catt became president of the National Suffrage Association, and she immediately injected new life into the old organization. She abandoned the effort to influence the states, in part because the liquor lobby was too strong at the local level, and changed tactics. She announced a six-year campaign for achieving an amendment to the Federal Constitution that would extend the vote to women. American entry into the war in 1917 speeded up her timetable. Women's participation in every facet of the war effort took them outside the home and demonstrated their initiative and adaptability, thus undermining the classic arguments against suffrage. From Catt at the national level to Ada James in Wisconsin, they contended that women's suffrage would demonstrate to the world America's commitment to democracy and reveal its superiority to German autocracy.

In January 1918 President Wilson yielded to these arguments and endorsed the suffrage amendment. His influence helped secure the two-thirds vote that the amendment needed in both houses of Congress, and it was submitted to the states on June 4, 1919. Just six days later Wisconsin and Illinois became the first states to ratify the amendment, and it went into effect in less than 14 months, in time to allow women to participate in the presidential election of 1920. In that election women joined men in throwing out the Wilsonian Democrats and in electing a conservative Republican, Warren G. Harding, to the presidency, along with a Republican majority in Congress. Carrie Catt and other leaders of the suffrage movement were the most disappointed that the ballot had failed to have a "social feminist" impact on American politics. Yet obtaining the vote was the forerunner of more profound social changes that would affect the role and status of women in the ensuing decade. Like prohibition, the "flapper" is another story.

▼

Progressives Oppose the League of Nations

If the success of the temperance and women's suffrage movements conveyed an impression to anyone that Progressivism had survived the war, the fight over American entry into the League of Nations in 1919-1920 quashed the notion. The idea of a postwar world organization had cropped up during the war, and politicians of all parties had endorsed it. A League of Nations was a cardinal feature of President Wilson's "Fourteen Points" speech of January 1918, in which he outlined a generous settlement with the Central Powers, a "peace without victory" that would forestall future wars. The League of Nations, then, was Progressivism writ large; the United States would make the world safe for the "Wisconsin idea."

The peace conference that brought a formal end to the war met in the royal palace at Versailles outside Paris in the spring of 1919. President Wilson attended the conference at the head of an American delegation one thousand strong, most of them scholarly experts on the geography, history and politics of Europe. In addition to imposing penalties on Germany for starting the war, the conference rearranged the map of Europe and created independent national republics in Eastern Europe out of what had once been the Dual Monarchy of Austria-Hungary.

At the insistence of the Americans, the Peace Treaty incorporated the charter for a League of Nations. Wilson envisioned the league as a mutual security agreement among the nations of the earth aimed at the two powers that were not represented in the conference or the league—Germany and the Soviet Union. Unfortunately, the league failed to address the one question that was most likely to upset world tranquillity: the demands for independence by proud peoples held in subjugation by the European powers—India, Egypt, the East Indies, Indo-China, parts of Africa.

The Versailles Treaty was published in the United States in

May 1919, and President Wilson began a yearlong struggle to secure its approval by the United States Senate. He was never able to secure the necessary two-thirds majority. There were several reasons why the treaty went down to defeat and the United States never joined the League of Nations—Republican partisanship, Wilson's own intransigent refusal to compromise and public indifference. But most interesting was the opposition of a band of Progressives led by Robert La Follette. Many senators of both parties would have accepted the League of Nations with certain modest changes in its charter, but La Follette and other "unreconcilables" would have none of it under any conditions. His reasons were those of the insurgent Progressive.

La Follette was not an isolationist; he had long believed in international cooperation. His objection to the covenant for the League of Nations, as drafted at Versailles, was that it was a reactionary document designed to preserve the hegemony of Britain, France and other imperial powers by suppressing movements for popular democracy that were erupting around the world in the war's aftermath. He complained that "The little group of men who sat ... at Versailles were not peacemakers. They were warmakers. They cut and slashed the map of the Old World. ... They locked the chains on the subject peoples of Ireland, Egypt, and India. ... then, fearing the wrath of outraged peoples, ... they made a league of nations to stand guard over the swag." While the Senate was considering amendments ("reservations") that would make the treaty palatable to the needed majority, La Follette introduced changes of his own. He would have granted colonies the right of revolution, demanded that all league members abolish military conscription and cut arms spending by 80 percent, required a referendum as a prelude to war, and prohibited the exploitation of the natural resources of weaker countries. All of his amendments were resoundingly defeated, finding no support among either Wilsonian Democrats or anti-treaty Republicans.

The votes of La Follette and three other insurgents delivered the death blow to the treaty and American participation in the League of Nations. Yet the real culprit was the American people who had grown entirely indifferent to the fate of the treaty by the time of the final Senate vote in the spring of 1920. Americans were tired of clarion calls to reform and world preservation, tired of Wilson's preaching, tired of shortages and restraints, eager for a return to "normalcy." La Follette's organization was in solid control of Wisconsin. He would run for president once more, in 1924, the year before he died, and his sons would keep his principles alive for another two and a half decades. But La Follette's brand of insurgency was dead by 1920, ironically sharing a grave with Wilsonian Progressivism. A new age had begun.

▼

Travelers' Guide

Wisconsin State Capitol, Capitol Square, Madison; (608) 266-0382. Completed in 1917, the Capitol building features Corinthian columns, marble floors, huge murals and a spectacular dome. Tours are offered daily.

Wisconsin Veterans Museum, 30 W. Mifflin St., Madison; (608) 264-6086. Includes exhibits illustrating the role of Wisconsin soldiers in World War I.

Chapter 7

OUR
TIMES

The defining characteristics of the 1920s begin with the letter "p": prosperity, prohibition and the pursuit of pleasure. Two of the three were indirect results of the Progressive movement. Prohibition, a product of the Progressives' temperance crusade, kept the country legally dry from the passage of the Volstead Act in 1919 until the repeal of the 18th Amendment in 1933. Women's suffrage, another Progressive reform, had little political impact on the 1920s, but it encouraged women to take a more assertive role socially. The new woman, or "flapper," * contributed to the impression of a fun-loving decade. Abetting the pursuit of pleasure were new entertainment technologies, the radio and motion pictures. A sports craze brought about the construction of huge stadiums and auditoriums. Camp Randall stadium in Madison, built in 1916 with a capacity of about 18,000, was constantly enlarged until it held 30,000 by 1930. The automobile, made available to the average wage earner by Henry Ford (the price of a Tin Lizzie in 1923 was $200), encouraged mobility, tourism and a flight from inner cities to the suburbs. Yet amid the prevalent prosperity there was a seamy side to American society. The popular evasion of the liquor laws helped finance crime in the cities. Prosperity eluded

---

* The origin of the term is unknown, but the most common guess is that it referred to a young bird just learning to fly.

farmers in Wisconsin and elsewhere. Labor unions were moribund. Wages remained fairly stable over the 10-year period, while man-hour production increased exponentially. The result was hefty corporate profits and a boom in the stock market. At the end of the decade, the structural flaws in the economy would erase the good times and plunge the nation into the worst depression in its history.

▼

Repeal of Prohibition

In 1930 an instructor in the university's new Letters and Science Experimental College asked his students to write term papers on the topic "The Prohibition Question." A student from Viroqua opened his discussion with the statement: "There is no Prohibition question in Viroqua. There can't be. There is no Prohibition." Supporting his thesis with lurid detail, the student listed 51 individuals and establishments engaged in selling liquor in the community. With typical small-town familiarity, he described some of the village's chief tipplers. As to Clarence: "Put a couple of cloves in his nose and it would be mistaken for a ham." Harold had eyes "like a couple of fried eggs." And Skinny best served as Viroqua's "standing argument for prohibition" because his one great ambition was "to get as drunk as he can as quick as he can and stay that way as long as he can." Nevertheless, Viroqua had no speakeasies, despite the availability of strong drink: "If you should happen by a dispensary and hear the wassail, lusty songs and feminine laughter that is always in evidence, speakeasy is the last term you would think of."

The student certainly exaggerated the level of inebriation in Viroqua. In that same year a federal commission named by President Herbert Hoover listed Vernon County, of which Viroqua is the seat, as officially "dry." More telling is the commission's finding that Vernon was one of only 20 counties (of a total of 71) that deserved to be called "dry." Wisconsin people were skeptical of the temperance experiment from the beginning, in part because "teetotalism," which prohibited even beer and wine, was too extreme. Commented one suburban newspaper editor, "A beerless Milwaukee is like a beanless Boston—it can't be done. Milwaukeeans will have their favorite beverage even if they have to brew it themselves." In 1921 a congressman from Sheboygan complained that the only effect of the Volstead Act was to manufacture "a vast number of liars and law violators."

Despite the evidence of widespread disobedience, Prohibition was not an utter failure. There was a decided decline in production and consumption of alcohol. The large breweries in Wisconsin shifted to nonalcoholic products, making use of their name advantage. Most of the smaller breweries simply closed their doors. Nationwide evidence suggests that liquor consumption during the 1920s was the lowest it had been since taxes and other restrictions were first imposed on distillers and retailers in the 1850s. Dissatisfaction with the law was nonetheless real. In a 1926 referendum Wisconsin voted overwhelmingly to amend the Volstead Act to permit the manufacture and sale of beer.

Celebrating the end of prohibition. Engine #8027 ready to move the first beer out of the Schlitz Brewery at 12:01 a.m., April 7, 1933.

In 1929 Wisconsin's voters repealed the state Prohibition enforcement law, leaving all enforcement of the temperance experiment to national "G-Men."

In 1926 La Follette protege John J. Blaine left the governorship and won a seat in the U.S. Senate on a pledge to implement the popular opinion expressed in the referendum of that year. He served only one term in the Senate, but before he left office he introduced a constitutional amendment repealing Prohibition. The measure swept through the Congress and went to the states for ratification by specially elected conventions. The 21st Amendment obtained the approval of two-thirds of the states in December 1933, and a nationwide celebration ensued. In Milwaukee raucous party-goers climbed all over the engine of the first train to leave the Schlitz brewery's shipping yards.

▼

Fight for Women's Rights Continues

The mood of conservatism that prevailed in the 1920s, reflected in the indifference of presidents Harding, Coolidge and Hoover to problems of poverty and unemployment, low farm prices and a growing gap between rich and poor, reinforced the feeling that granting women the vote made no difference in the political order of things. Feminist leaders, such as Carrie Chapman Catt who had formed the League of Women Voters to familiarize both male and female voters with the important issues of the day, were the most bitterly disappointed of all. Jane Addams, one of the leading advocates of "social feminism" before the war, remarked bitterly that women in public office were distinguished chiefly by their eagerness to vote for military budgets and war. (Not entirely true. Jeanette Rankin of Montana was the only member of Congress to vote against war in both 1917 and 1941.)

Whatever might have happened nationally, the women of Wisconsin did not scurry back to home and hearth when the 19th Amendment went into effect. Sensing that the feminists were still a political force, John J. Blaine campaigned for governor in 1920 on a platform that promised equality for women in all phases of society. The following spring the Legislature considered a bill to clarify women's rights. As originally drafted, the bill promised blanket equality, before the law and in job occupations. It instantly ran into the white-haired argument of social disintegration. "Our civilization is tottering and crumbling and I think we should go slow in passing this kind of legislation," cautioned an assemblyman. "This bill will result in coarsening the fibre of women—it takes her out of her proper sphere." Unfortunately, women themselves were divided on the virtues of the measure. Social feminists, who had obtained special limits on the working hours of women during the reform era, worried that equality might be a step backward. To satisfy this objection, the Legislature exempted protective regulations for women, and the compromise bill passed both houses. The compromise was not acceptable to the leaders of the National Woman's Party (founded in 1916), which began work on an Equal Rights Amendment to the U.S. Constitution. The ERA was still foundering on the hoary argument of social disintegration 70 years later.

The Wisconsin League of Women Voters opposed the equal rights concept out of a La Follette-style fear that corporate business would use it to reduce both men and women to the status of an industrial proletariat. But, in alliance with La Follette Progressives, the league did gain recognition of a number of civic rights and responsibilities. In 1921 the Legislature allowed women to serve on juries. The following year the league persuaded the University Extension to begin offering a course for the training of policewomen on grounds that policewomen were needed for the protection of children in the streets. Such efforts were nevertheless limited, in part because of the low turnout of women at the polls and the reluctance of women to run for public office. Only four women served in the Wisconsin Legislature during the 1920s, and only two lasted more than a single term.

▼

Agriculture Advances

At the end of the war Wisconsin farmers and businessmen looked to the future with immense optimism. Europe was shattered, economically and physically. Large portions of France had been reduced to a wasteland; Germany and Central Europe were in political and social chaos. Britain was all but bankrupt. It appeared that

Europe would be dependent on American cereal grains and industrial products for years, perhaps decades. And, indeed, there was a postwar boom, spurred in part by agricultural exports. But a market panic in late 1920 brought an abrupt end to the good times, and a sharp but brief recession followed. The economy righted itself by 1923, and the nation embarked on a period of prosperity that lasted until the end of the decade. The prosperity was spotty, however, and among those who failed to share in it were Wisconsin's dairy farmers. European agriculture recovered more quickly than anyone had expected, and the farm machinery purchased during the war enhanced production and contributed to the crop surpluses. American farmers faced a problem familiar since the 1870s—they produced, in the normal course of events, more grain, beef and dairy products than the available market could consume.

Although science could do nothing about crop surpluses and low prices, the university's College of Agriculture continued its pioneering research in the field of nutrition. In the 1890s Stephen M. Babcock, carrying on the experiments of Dean William A. Henry in milk production, devised an easy test for determining the butterfat content of milk. Babcock declined to patent his invention, feeling that discoveries by university scientists ought to be freely available to all. When Dean Henry retired in 1907, President Van Hise and the university regents named Harry L. Russell Dean of the College of Agriculture. Although chiefly interested in theoretical research, Russell agreed with the direction taken by the college and supported the idea of practical applications that would directly benefit the farmers of the state.

Babcock, given a research team by Dean Russell, became convinced, through his experiments with cattle feeds, that there must exist some as yet undiscovered element necessary to growth, if not to life itself. After patient experimentation, a member of Babcock's team, E.V. McCollum, isolated a chemical compound that controlled growth. He announced his discovery in 1913, calling it "fat-soluble A." Soon thereafter McCollum identified yet another food component that affected an animal's health and labeled it "water-soluble B." Further experiments in America and Europe led to the use of the term "vitamins" to describe food components necessary to the life and health of most animals.

A decade later Harry Steenbock, another member of Babcock's original team, discovered a way to produce yet another vitamin, D, through radiation. He instantly faced the dilemma of whether to patent the discovery. It had tremendous commercial potential, for the vitamin could be an important additive to milk. Steenbock feared that if he did not apply for a patent his process could be mishandled and abused. That is precisely what had happened to Babcock's butterfat test. Without a patent, Babcock had no way of controlling the dairy industry's use of the test. Unscrupulous marketers made wild claims for the butterfat content of their products, and the test itself came into disrepute. On the other hand, if Steenbock obtained a patent he would be violating the principle of public service to which the university was committed and gaining personal enrichment out of university resources.

Researchers in other institutions faced the same dilemma, and a Chicago law firm had worked out the idea of an independent foun-

An early snowmobile, 1921, invented by Gilbert V. King of Germania. His vehicles were purchased by doctors and rural mail carriers in the Princeton area.

dation, financed by patent royalties and devoted to the welfare of the university. Steenbock obtained a patent on his radiation process and worked with university authorities to create a foundation managed by trustees who were alumni but had no other connection with the university. The regents approved the idea, and the Wisconsin Alumni Research Foundation (WARF) was incorporated in 1925. The foundation prospered on university research patents, and during the hard times of the 1930s it was almost the only source of funding for faculty research.

The most distressed part of the state during the booming '20s was the cutover, the northern half that had been stripped of its forest cover in the logging days. The lumber companies made no effort to restore the landscape; instead they moved on to exploit the fir-laden mountains of the Pacific Northwest and the long-leaf pine uplands of the South. Before the war La Follette Progressives encouraged people to take up farming in the cutover, but most farming enterprises failed. The glacial drift was infertile and did not retain water. The

The effects of agricultural extension education. Contour plowing and the rotation of crops in strips at the Elmer Hanske farm near Chaseburg.

removal of tree stumps was a nightmarish job that required more money and effort than the returns from the land justified.

Wisconsin's North Woods, a lovely land of crystalline lakes, bountiful wildlife and verdant new-growth forests, had long attracted wealthy visitors. They came by train and settled into comfortable hotels and resorts, but they were too few to afford an economic base for the north country. The automobile brought another kind of tourist, the "gypsy" who brought his own tent and camped by the roadside or in a farmer's field. These tourists were considered a nuisance at first because they broke fences and littered the landscape, but the people of the North soon recognized their commercial potential. "The tourist crop," observed the *New North* of Rhinelander in 1923, was fast becoming "one of the most profitable crops raised in the state." Every summer brought increasing numbers of vacationers. Hotels expanded, and one-time farmers set up lakeside resorts and private campgrounds. The summer visitors kept coming even through the financially depressed 1930s, offering future hope that northern Wisconsin, whose chief resource was placid beauty, would somehow survive.

▼

Retreat From Progressivism

Bob La Follette firmly believed that World War I had "openly enthroned Big Business in mastery of government." Sacrificing principle to the needs of production, the Wilson administration removed antitrust barriers and encouraged manufacturers to pool their products and fix their prices. At the end of the war, businessmen fought hard to preserve their noncompetitive habits, and they received support from the Supreme Court, which declined to break up monopolistic corporations unless they "unreasonably" restrained trade. Early in his administration, Warren Harding invited J.P. Morgan and other financiers to the White House for advice, the first such public collaboration since the 1890s. Harding announced that he favored "more business in government and less government in business." He thus set the tone for the politics of the 1920s, in the nation and in Wisconsin.

The retreat from Progressivism was not immediately evident in Wisconsin because the La Follette name and organization remained a political force. John J. Blaine, a La Follette protege, served as governor from 1921 to 1927, and the state's electoral vote went to La Follette's maverick presidential candidacy in 1924. When "Fighting Bob" died the following year, Robert La Follette Jr. was elected to fill his Senate seat and would hold it for the next 22 years. The drift into conservatism became evident in 1926 when Republican Stalwarts, backed by officials from the Nash Motor Company (formed in Kenosha the previous year) and General Motors (which had built a Chevrolet assembly plant in Janesville) backed Fred Zimmerman for governor. Although Zimmerman had served as a La Follette delegate to the Republican national conventions in 1916, 1920 and 1924, the Stalwarts correctly perceived him to be a glad-hander without political convictions and only a superficial knowledge of the issues. In 1928 the Stalwarts abandoned the facade and chose a businessman for their gubernatorial candidate, Walter J. Kohler, a manufacturer of plumbing equipment from Sheboygan who had kept unions out of his shop by building a model company town for his employees. In addition to electing Kohler, Wisconsin gave its electoral vote to Herbert Hoover in that presidential election year.

One result of the pro-business climate of the 1920s was the decline of organized labor. Labor unions, under the national umbrella of the American Federation of Labor, had made giant strides before the war, but after the war employers across the nation formed organizations to assure the open (i.e., nonunionized) shop in law and in practice. Although the open shop served their interests, their position was not entirely hypocritical. They believed they were supporting the constitutional right of workingmen to join organizations of their choosing, and they urged cooperation and understanding between employer and employee. "Labor requires capital and capital requires labor," observed the president of the Marshall and Ilsley Bank of Milwaukee, who thought the antagonism would disappear when both sides understood this truth. Most employers accepted such advice as the voice of reason, but they tended to think that it was the trade unions that needed lessons in good will and reciprocal concessions.

Organized labor added to its difficulties. It adhered to a trade-union ideology—the organization of skilled craftsmen—and it was slow to accept innovations, such as the automobile assembly line where little or no skill was required. The new assembly plants attracted workers from rural areas who had no familiarity with unions and who were conditioned to the gospel of self-help. A single statistic exemplifies the trend. In 1933, when Phillip La Follette completed his first term as governor, union membership in the city of Milwaukee was at the same level it had been when his father won his first gubernatorial election in 1900.

▼

Wisconsin Faces the Depression

The stock market crash of 1929 did not cause panic in Wisconsin. The Antigo *Daily Journal* thought that the Federal Reserve System, created by Woodrow Wilson in 1913, would prevent the sort of banking panic that the nation had experienced periodically in the 19th century. It echoed President Hoover's assessment that the nation's business was fundamentally sound and asserted that "there should be no confusing of Wall Street with 'Main Street.'" The profits of stock market speculators, suggested the Appleton *Post-Crescent*, had as little relationship to the nation's prosperity as the profits from a poker game. "After a card game," the paper pointed out, "there is just as much money in the room as there was before. It is merely distributed differently. It is the same with operations on the stock exchange." These appraisals were not wholly wrong; they merely failed to take into account the panic's psychological effect on business investment and consumer purchases. The stock market panic worsened a downward spiral in the economy that was already underway. Surplus goods, lowered production, layoffs, unemployment and consumer parsimony followed one another into the maelstrom.

President Herbert Hoover, whose book *Rugged Individualism* earlier in the decade had earned him the title of apostle of free enterprise, was certain that the economy could right itself without government intervention. Gov. Kohler was of like mind. As statistics of unemployment flowed into the executive office, Kohler returned to the idea of cooperation. He formed a citizens' committee to conduct a survey of the state to determine in which areas jobs were plentiful so that people without jobs could be directed to them. The committee was still carrying on its "educational work" when Phillip Fox La Follette, "Fighting Bob" 's elder son, replaced Kohler as governor in 1930.

In characteristic La Follette fashion, Phillip began by collecting information on how other states and countries were handling the problem of unemployment. Important advice came from Edwin Witte, a University of Wisconsin economist (later the author of the federal Social Security Act) who had accompanied a team of experts sent abroad by the Carnegie Fund. Witte advised adoption of government-financed unemployment insurance modeled on the British system, while cautioning that a variety of programs, including public works, would be needed to get a significant number of people back to work.

La Follette called the Legislature into special session on November 24, 1931, and asked for a series of measures to provide relief for the unemployed. In addition to unemployment compensation, he called for expansion of electric power construction proj-ects and the use of state agencies to help private businesses recover productivity. Diagnosing the nation's troubles as the result of inequitable distribution of income, the governor opined that taxation was "an effective instrument with which to redistribute money to enable farmers and workers to trade with one another." The address caught national attention. Felix Frankfurter (later to be named to the Supreme Court) wrote from the Harvard Law School to congratulate the 30-year-old governor for having produced "the most heartening state paper that has come out of the depression." Historian Charles A. Beard (a specialist on the Founding Fathers and a lifelong Republican) enthused: "In all the history of American public documents there has not appeared a more important or more reasoned state paper." La Follette had tapped a growing realization among scholars, politicians and even businessmen that the economic crisis required a new look at the fundamentals of American capitalism.

At the beginning of his term La Follette had formed a committee to study unemployment in the state and draft a compensation bill. Two of John R. Commons' students played key roles on the committee—Paul Raushenbush, son of a prominent theologian whose social gospel movement in the 1890s had anticipated Progressivism, and Paul's wife Elizabeth Brandeis, daughter of Justice Louis Brandeis. Utilizing Commons' methods, they won support from the state's farm organizations as well as organized labor. With employer opposition neutralized, the Legislature quickly approved the measure, and in January 1932 Gov. La Follette signed into law the first unemployment compensation act in the country. The Legislature also approved

Line of people registering for unemployment compensation in Milwaukee City Hall, 1932, after the Wisconsin Legislature passed its pioneering law.

public works projects, such as the improvement of railroad-grade crossings, and a forestry program for northern Wisconsin, financed through a surtax on incomes and a tax on stock dividends.

Wisconsin's response to the Depression became a model for other states. "It is one of the happy incidents of the federal system," wrote Justice Brandeis in a Supreme Court opinion later that year, "that a single courageous State may, if its citizens choose, serve as a laboratory; and try novel social and economic experiments without risk to the rest of the country." His daughter echoed the sentiment. "It was a thrilling experience," Elizabeth later wrote, "to live in Wisconsin in these years, to feel that there was a program under way, that government was playing a constructive part, that real things were being planned and done."

Stalwarts in the Republican Part heartily disagreed. In 1932 Kohler defeated Phil La Follette in the Republican primary. Both La Follettes promptly threw their support to Franklin Roosevelt in the presidential contest, and Roosevelt carried the state. It was the first time Wisconsin had voted Democratic in a presidential election since 1912 and only the third time since it obtained statehood. Roosevelt recognized his debt to Wisconsin's Progressives and frequently sought advice from both of the La Follettes.

In the Senate Robert La Follette supported most of the legislation of the New Deal's hectic Hundred Days in the spring of 1933. However, he disapproved of Roosevelt's tendency to finance his relief programs by borrowing, rather than taxation. Having diagnosed the Depression as caused by maldistribution of wealth, Robert thought it could be cured with a graduated income tax. He clearly had no comprehension of Keynsian economics, but, then, Roosevelt himself did not embrace the principle of deficit spending until 1935.

The Civilian Conservation Corps was the earliest—and in the long run one of the most effective—of the New Deal's relief agencies. By July 1933, three months after it was established, the CCC had enrolled 250,000 young men and put them to work in 1,300 camps throughout the nation. In its nine-year existence the CCC put to work 92,000 men in Wisconsin carrying out conservation projects in 45 camps. Most of the camps were located in national and state forests where the primary work was tree planting and erosion control. To help combat forest fires the CCC built nearly 4,000 miles of fire lanes and forest trails. Living in a military regimen, the

CCC boys (age 17 to 25) received $5 a month for themselves and $25 for their families back home. The chief flaw in the organization was racial bias. Over the objections of both of the La Follette brothers, the CCC sent the state's black volunteers to a segregated camp in Illinois.

The CCC and other early relief efforts of the New Deal were of benefit chiefly to the urban unemployed. The farm program of the early New Deal was an ill-conceived bust. It was based on the idea of destroying crops in order to create shortages ("induced scarcity") that

The Milk Strike, January 1934. Strikers stopped a train outside Burlington by throwing tires across the track. They broke open seven cars carrying milk and dumped the cans.

would raise prices. It brought only national derision and had less effect on the farm surpluses than the drought and "dust bowl" of 1934. Even before the program could be put into effect Wisconsin's dairymen in the spring of 1933 experimented with the principal of induced scarcity on their own. The price of milk had dropped from two dollars a hundredweight in 1929 to less than a dollar by 1932. Farmers were unable to meet their mortgage payments and faced the prospect of becoming tenants on their own lands. Adopting one of the methods that big business used to control supply, the dairymen formed a Milk Pool, and they threatened to withhold milk from the market until prices improved. In February 1933 pool members in the Fox River Valley went on strike. They closed down several cheese and butter factories and barricaded the roads leading to city markets. When the governor called out the National Guard, they adopted guerilla tactics, seizing unprotected trucks on the highway, spilling the milk onto the roadway, and scattering in cars before the Guard could arrive. The strike was too localized to have any impact on dairy prices, and by June, when the New Deal's Agricultural Adjustment Administration began operation, the strike had petered out. The AAA's limitations on milk production improved prices slightly, but it was far from a permanent solution.

Robert La Follette was up for re-election to the Senate in 1934, and Phillip harbored ambitions of returning to the governor's chair. Neither stood much chance of Republican support, for the breathtaking pace of the New Deal had solidified the Stalwarts' control of the GOP. The Democratic Party was not an attractive alternative because Wisconsin Democrats, true to their Bourbon heritage, had misgivings about the New Deal. A third party seemed the only alternative. A convention at Fond du Lac, with delegates from farmer and labor organizations, Socialists and the La Follette faithful, adopted the name Progressive. The new party nominated Robert for the Senate and Phillip for the governorship. President Roosevelt visited Wisconsin during the election and warmly praised Sen. La Follette, though he had nary a word to say on behalf of brother Phil. (Roosevelt may have begun to mistrust Phillip, who had never hidden his ambition for national office.) With the help of liberal

Democrats, the Progressives carried the state in the fall election, returning both brothers to office, electing seven of the state's 10 congressmen, and capturing a good block of seats in the Legislature.

In 1935, with the nation's economy mired in depression as deeply as ever, President Roosevelt asked Congress for an immense and semipermanent appropriation for unemployment relief. He set up a new alphabet agency, the Works Progress Administration (WPA), to spend the money and create jobs. Although the WPA was the subject of much derision ("We Piddle Around"), Phillip La Follette made good use of it in Wisconsin. He approached the Roosevelt administration with a comprehensive plan for state development and obtained a lump sum grant of $100 million earmarked for Wisconsin alone. The money was spent on soil conservation and erosion control, fish and game management, reforestation, highway construction and urban renewal. In the election of 1936 Roosevelt easily swept the state, with almost 75 percent of the vote, and La Follette was re-elected with important help from heavily Democratic Milwaukee, Racine and Kenosha counties.

Although he won re-election, Phillip La Follette's career began to come unglued in 1936. His own unbridled ambition was the root of it. He could not brook any competition from within the ranks of Progressives. When he discovered that university president Glenn Frank harbored political ambitions of his own, La Follette utilized a statutory loophole to rearrange the board of regents. The new board asked for Frank's resignation, and when he refused to leave, it voted to dismiss him. The blatant political interference in the affairs of the university aroused nationwide criticism. The following year people associated La Follette's heavy-handedness with Roosevelt's unfortunate attempt to "pack" the Supreme Court. By the end of 1937 the Progressive Party was showing serious fissures. Yet La Follette plunged on, using every ounce of executive influence to ram a government reorganization act through the Legislature. The legislative session ended amid boos and catcalls, with both Republicans and Democrats mimicking the Nazi salute and chanting "Heil."

La Follette assumed that in 1940 Roosevelt would defer to the tradition established by George Washington and retire after serving

Aldo Leopold, father of environmentalism, on his Sand County farm.

two terms in office. He organized a national Progressive Party in 1938 and broke publicly with Roosevelt. In a series of nationwide radio addresses La Follette criticized the New Deal for a patchwork approach to the Depression that had failed to solve the nation's economic crisis. He promised to revive the economy by stimulating production rather than inducing scarcity. As fate would have it, Roosevelt himself endorsed that principle in his so-called "Third New Deal" of 1938, and liberals had trouble distinguishing La Follette's ideas from those of FDR. They also worried that a split among liberals would open the way for a Republican victory in 1940.

Nothing went right for Phillip that year. Wisconsin voters reacted negatively to the idea of a new national party—when they bothered to think about it at all. Personal tragedy added to the governor's woes. In March, a month before La Follette's open break with Roosevelt, Tom Duncan, the governor's ablest political adviser, killed a man in a hit-and-run accident. The police report indicated that Duncan had been drinking and did not even know that he had struck someone. Because of the political sensitivity of the case, it was decided that Duncan should be tried before a judge imported from Ashland, locally respected for his independence and integrity, Gulick N. Risjord (the author's grandfather). The judge heard the case and found Duncan guilty of first-degree manslaughter. However, he imposed a comparatively light sentence of only one to two years in prison, probably because Duncan had no other criminal record. The sentence proved politically damaging to the governor, who was accused of favoritism as he stumped the state in the fall election. La Follette lost the election to a Republican regular, and he never held public office again.

▼

World War II

The La Follette brothers both opposed American entry into World War II, just as their father had opposed the first world war. Their rationale differed from their father's, however. La Follette Sr. had seen World War I as a contest of decadent monarchies in which the United States had no vital interest. The La Follette brothers conceded the threat of fascism in 1940 as Nazi armies marched across Europe. But they contended, as did the America First Committee, that the vast resources needed to defeat fascism abroad were better used to promote peaceful enterprise at home. A strong domestic economy was the surest safeguard against fascism in the long run, they thought, and war ran the risk of calamity. "With the enormous debt the world now carries and with the awful increase in the destructiveness of war today," Phil asserted, "you can write it down as a foregone conclusion, that if this is a prolonged war, it will end in the complete collapse of the economic and political systems of every nation which participates in it."

In the Senate, Robert was still fighting the Depression in 1941. He opposed military conscription and objected to the deflection of funds from the WPA to national defense. Nevertheless, after the Japanese attacked Pearl Harbor the senator muted his criticism of the war effort, and he concentrated on the character of the postwar world. In 1944-45 he heartily embraced American participation in the United Nations, and he approved the formation of an International Monetary Fund and a World Bank. By the end of the war Robert La Follette Jr. was viewed as an elder statesman, credited with keeping alive the idealism of his father and reshaping it to meet the needs of a modern world. The Wisconsin Idea, enthused *Life* magazine, "is a far purer and more consistent body of radical doctrine than was the New Deal, being built not only on social welfare, but on a deep faith in small business, equal opportunity, and individual freedom. It is a peculiarly American kind of radicalism, free from all taint of 'foreign ideologies.' "

Although he had been elected as a Progressive in 1934 and 1940, Robert decided, on the basis of his long record in the Senate, to run as a Republican in 1946. Unfortunately, he did not have time to campaign for the party's primary. The most important issue before Congress that year was government reorganization, trimming the ragged edges of the New Deal and eliminating waste and duplication. Work on the bill kept Robert in Washington until 10 days before the election. In a light voter turnout, Robert lost the nomination by a scant 5,000 votes. The winner, a political newcomer: Joseph R. McCarthy.

▼

Joseph R. McCarthy

His grandfather had migrated from Ireland and carved out a farm in the Fox River Valley near Appleton in the 1840s. Joe McCarthy had an Irishman's sense of camaraderie and gift for the tall tale. Blessed with a photographic memory and unbridled ambition, he seemed destined for fame, or at least notoriety. With hard work and a faculty for memorization, he performed four years of high school classwork in a single year, taking advantage of an experimental program that allowed students to work at their own pace. He rollicked through Marquette and its law school with fraternity parties and poker games. (His favorite tactic in poker was to bet an enormous sum and then scoop up the pot when the other players folded.) In 1939, after only three years of law practice, he was elected a circuit judge in Shawano. When World War II broke out he obtained a commission as a lieutenant in the Marines and was assigned to a dive bomber squadron in the South Pacific. Expecting to use his war record as a springboard for higher political office, he put a sign, "HEADQUARTERS, McCARTHY FOR U.S. SENATE," across his tent. Although his duties were confined to debriefing pilots, he persuaded friends to take him on "milk run" missions, and he had himself photographed in the "tailgunner" seat of a bomber.

In 1944 McCarthy obtained a leave of absence from the Marines and entered the Republican primary against Sen. Alexander Wiley. He financed the campaign with profits from a lucky investment on the stock market (and on which he failed to pay an income tax). There was some confusion among the voters because he had been elected a judge as a Democrat. (He once confided to a friend that he had voted for Franklin Roosevelt three times.) He lost the election but surprised the senator with his electoral strength, due in part to Democratic crossovers. Two years later he ran against Robert La Follette and won. He then went on to defeat the Democratic candidate in the general election. His war record, including his "wound" (which in fact was incurred when he slipped off a ladder during a party) was only part of the reason for the victory. 1946 was a year of rising international tensions, as the wartime alliance broke apart and the Soviet Union took an increasingly belligerent stance toward the West. Republican candidates across the country were accusing Roosevelt and Truman of being "soft on communism," meaning that they were not tough enough with the Soviet Union and insufficiently alert to the Communist menace at home. McCarthy quickly learned, in debates with his Democratic opponent, how useful Red Scare tactics could be. The *Capital Times* of Madison had exposed the curious finances of his 1944 campaign against Sen. Wiley, and when his opponent brought up the subject, McCarthy counterattacked with suggestions of his adversary's disloyalty. McCarthy alleged that the Communist *Daily Worker* regarded the Democrat (a New Deal congressman and political science lecturer at the University of Wisconsin) to be a fellow traveler. "Meaning a Communist," McCarthy explained. That placed his opponent on the defensive and sidetracked the entire debate. It was a lesson McCarthy never forgot.

In the Senate McCarthy joined a group of conservative Republicans who blamed President Truman for "allowing" eastern Europe to be swept into the Soviet orbit and China to fall into Communist hands. In the House of Representatives, the Un-American Activities Committee, spearheaded by Richard Nixon, began looking for Communists in the American government. Truman responded by ordering a loyalty check of all government employees. The House committee eventually identified an ex-Communist, Alger Hiss, and when Hiss denied the charge he was convicted of perjury in January 1950. A month later McCarthy set out to make a series of Lincoln Day speeches sponsored by the Republican Party. The schedule was unexciting, as was appropriate for a little-known junior senator. It began in Wheeling, West Virginia, and ended in Huron, South Dakota. The only bright spots were stops in Reno and Las Vegas where McCarthy could indulge his love for gambling.

In Wheeling on February 9 McCarthy shocked the nation by waving a paper purporting to contain the names of 205 "Communists" in the State Department. Across the country Republican orators were blaming the worldwide advance of communism on "traitors" in the American foreign service, but McCarthy was the first to claim a list of names. The paper he waved was in fact a phony. It was a list, but only of people the State Department had decided not to hire four years earlier. It contained no mention of Communists.

Did McCarthy actually believe that he had uncovered Communists in the State Department? Probably not. After he returned to Washington he confided to reporters of *The Milwaukee Journal* that the Lincoln Day speeches were just "political." He also telephoned J. Edgar Hoover and said, "This caused headlines all over the country, and I never expected it, and now I need some evidence to back up my statement that there are Communists in the State Department." According to a close aide of the FBI director, Hoover was furious at the Wheeling speech and gave Joe "unshirted hell" for bluffing. Nevertheless, Hoover found McCarthy useful, and for years thereafter he supplied him with data from FBI files. As McCarthy went through this data and other information supplied him by right-wing groups across the country, a change came over him—a change observed by close friends. He became a true believer, convinced that the government—indeed, all of American society—was riddled with Communist traitors. And Americans were prepared to believe him. A series of sensational spy cases involving the release of atomic weapons information to the Soviet Union had people thoroughly spooked. On July 4, 1951, John Patrick Hunter, a young reporter for *The Capital Times,* went out onto the streets of Madison asking people to sign a petition containing the preamble to the Declaration of Independence and portions of the Bill of Rights. Of 112 people he asked to sign, all but one refused. Columnist Drew Pearson brought the incident to national attention. "That is McCarthyism," Pearson said, "a disease of fear—unreasoning fear, mortal fear, fear of ideas, fear of books, fear of the good old American right to sign a petition. And that disease is marching like a monster through the minds of its victims." McCarthy, who had long since begun referring to *The Capital Times* as the *Madison Daily Worker,* contended on the Senate floor that Communists on the paper had concocted the entire scheme.

With the Korean War at a stalemate and Truman's popularity at a record low, 1952 looked to be a Republican year, and it was McCarthy's good fortune that he was up for re-election. The Republicans nominated for president the hero of the war in Europe, Dwight D. Eisenhower, and it bowed to the Communist hunters by placing Richard Nixon on the ticket as vice president. Eisenhower detested McCarthy because of a speech Joe had made in the Senate denouncing Ike's friend, Gen. George Marshall, as part of "a conspiracy so immense as to dwarf any previous such venture in the history of man. A conspiracy of infamy so black that, when it is finally exposed, its principals shall be forever deserving of the maledictions of all honest men." Marshall had drawn the fire of conservative Republicans because, as Secretary of State in 1946-47, he had predicted that the Nationalists would lose the civil war in China and advised Truman to cut his losses.

When his campaign train chugged into Milwaukee in September 1952, Eisenhower inserted a strong defense of Gen. Marshall in a speech he was scheduled to make with McCarthy on the platform. However, on the advice of aides that it would cost him votes in Wisconsin, Ike deleted the passage from the speech (although it remained in the printed version given to reporters). Were Eisenhower's aides correct? How powerful was McCarthy in Wisconsin? The election results are quite revealing. McCarthy was re-elected with 54 percent of the vote, which his supporters claimed was a "smashing victory." In fact, his total was more than 100,000 votes fewer than he had garnered in 1946. Of the 11 Republicans on the ticket, he ran last. He trailed Gov. Walter Kohler by 9 percent, the state's congressional delegation by 7.3 percent and Eisenhower by 7 percent. He failed to carry Madison or any of the lakeshore cities. McCarthy was re-elected by the traditionally Republican vote of rural Wisconsin. His Communist hunt made no difference. One analyst concluded that, but for Eisenhower's landslide, McCarthy would not have been re-elected.

Eisenhower's coattails gave the Republicans control of the Senate in 1953, and McCarthy became chair of a Permanent Subcommittee on Investigations. In the past the committee had investigated everything from trade policy to homosexuals in the government. No one, including McCarthy, was certain of the scope of its powers. Joe soon began speaking of extensive anti-Communist probes, including "Communist thinkers" in the nation's colleges. His staff began investgating the State Department's operations in Europe, its embassies and its Iron Curtain-directed radio station, the Voice of America.

The Senate was cooperative. The right-wing ruled the GOP; minority leader Lyndon Johnson claimed that McCarthy was the "Republicans' problem." The Eisenhower administration retreated from every confrontation, firing hundreds of State Department employees, eliminating some of the Voice of America's programs and closing overseas libraries. Then, at the height of his power, McCarthy overstepped himself. He took on an institution that no one in the country could reasonably believe was a hotbed of communism—the United States Army.

In the fall of 1953 he began investigating Communist infiltration at Signal Corps posts in New Jersey. The record-keeping at the posts, including the handling of classified materials, had been sloppy, a fact that the Army readily admitted, but there was no evidence of espionage. Even close friends of McCarthy were appalled at his brutal treatment of Army officers before his committee and advised him to back off. He declined, in part because of what one friendly analyst called "the velocity of events." Accusations poured in upon him, and he seemed eager to investigate them all. He raced around the country, indiscriminately accepting scores of invitations for

G. David Schine, Sen. McCarthy and Roy Cohn during the Army-McCarthy hearings in April 1954.

public speeches. He lost the ability to laugh at himself, a feature of his personality that had long charmed friends and relatives, and he lost the time to sit and pause for the most elementary reflection. He had also begun to drink heavily.

In March 1954, after McCarthy had berated Secretary of War Robert T. Stevens as a man under the influence of "the wrong elements" and an "awful dupe," the Army struck back. It released transcripts of the efforts of McCarthy's chief investigator, Roy Cohn, to obtain special treatment for an assistant that had been drafted. Even Republicans thought Cohn ought to resign. McCarthy recklessly went to the defense of his errant staff and called for open hearings on the subject. His subcommittee agreed, but since McCarthy himself was a party to the dispute, it placed Sen. Karl Mundt in the chair.

On the eve of the televised Army-McCarthy hearings, the Gallup Poll reported that 46 percent of those who were aware of the dispute believed Stevens and the Army; 23 percent sided with Joe. The hearings opened on April 22, 1954, and for the next eight weeks (with a short recess in May) the American public watched transfixed as McCarthy destroyed himself. There for all to see was the glowering bully, constantly interrupting the testimony by shouting "point of order," and leveling personal accusations against members of the Army's legal team.

Earlier that spring, 50-year-old Leroy Gore, editor of Sauk City's weekly *Sauk-Prairie Star* and a lifelong Republican, decided that "Joe Must Go." He began circulating 15,000 petitions to recall the senator and force him to face a new election. Under the law, Gore had to obtain 403,804 notarized signatures within a 60-day period. The "Joe Must Go" movement failed by a narrow margin, but McCarthy was finished anyway. In July Sen. Ralph Flanders, a Vermont Republican, introduced a resolution of censure. Vote on the resolution was delayed until after the fall election, but on December 2, 1954, the Senate voted by 67 to 22 to "condemn" McCarthy. Joe put on a bold front, telling reporters that he was "happy to have this circus ended so I can get back to the real work of digging out communism, crime and corruption." But his spirit was destroyed, and alcoholism slowly conquered him. He died in 1957 of massive liver failure.

In 1957 Wisconsin held a special election to fill McCarthy's seat in the Senate. The winner was William Proxmire, a Democrat who had moved to Wisconsin from Illinois in 1949 with a view to building a political career. In the early 1950s he helped to rebuild the state Democratic Party (in disarray since Roosevelt's day), while unsuccessfully contesting Walter Kohler for the governorship. In 1958 the voters returned Proxmire to the Senate for a term of his own, amid a nationwide repudiation of the Republican Old Guard.

Proxmire's victory marked the end of nearly 20 years of Republican rule in Wisconsin and inaugurated, for the first time in the state's history, a genuine two-party system. Democrat Gaylord Nelson won the governorship in 1958 and captured Alexander Wylie's Senate seat in 1962. He was twice re-elected to the Senate before yielding to Republican Robert Kasten in 1980, who was, in turn, defeated by Democrat Russ Feingold in 1992. Through the 1960s, '70s and '80s the two parties regularly exchanged control of the branches of the state government. In the 36 years bracketed by the elections of 1958 and 1994 each party held the governor's chair for 18 years. Control of the Assembly changed hands with equal regularity but not necessarily at the same time. The parties frequently had to share the responsibility of managing the government.

Perhaps because the parties were evenly matched, the political battles of the 1960s, '70s, '80s and '90s seemed to lack the intensity and significance of some of the epochal fights of earlier years. There were nevertheless moments when Wisconsin had an impact on the nation's destiny—Democratic primaries in 1960 and 1968 and the 1960s civil rights struggle in Milwaukee.

▼

The 1960 Democratic Primary

The contest for the Democratic nomination for president in 1960 boiled down to a two-way race between Sen. Hubert Humphrey of Minnesota, the choice of Roosevelt-Truman liberals, and Sen. John F. Kennedy of Massachusetts, whose voting record in

Congress was so ill-defined that he had supporters in all bands of the political spectrum. Because the ideological differences between the two were so fuzzy, religion became a major issue in the campaign. Kennedy was a Catholic, and no Catholic had ever been elected president of the United States. Al Smith, the only Catholic nominated by a major party, had been smothered by Herbert Hoover in 1928. Kennedy won an early primary victory over Humphrey in West Virginia, but it meant little because the Minnesota senator was virtually unknown in that Allegheny mountain state.

Although the idea of the direct primary was more than a half-century old, few states had meaningful primaries in 1960. The candidates were thus free to choose which ones to contest. Wisconsin, whose March primary was relatively early, was their first important battleground. With its sizable concentration of Catholic German, Slavic and Irish voters, Wisconsin was a good choice for Kennedy. Although no Catholic had ever been elected governor of the state, Catholics had been elected to the Legislature, the Supreme Court and the Congress. Joe McCarthy was a Catholic, and in neither of his elections was religion an issue.

In the primary Kennedy resoundingly defeated Humphrey and propelled himself into the presidential nomination. Although Catholics voted overwhelmingly for Kennedy, religion, interestingly enough, was not the sole factor in his victory. The Kennedy family had close ties with Joe McCarthy, which undoubtedly helped the candidate in the Appleton-Green Bay area. Joe Kennedy, the family patriarch, had discovered a Communist "menace" even before World War II. After McCarthy was elected to the Senate, the Kennedys frequently entertained him at their Hyannisport home, where he broke a rib playing "touch" football. When McCarthy became chair of the Senate Committee on Investigations, he gave young Robert Kennedy a job as investigator. Republicans, even those with no loyalty to the memory of McCarthy, crossed over to vote for Kennedy in the Democratic primary, a move that was legal at the time. They clearly perceived him as the more conservative of the two. Even so, the Republican vote was a short-term tactic. In the fall election Richard Nixon carried Wisconsin.

▼

Civil Rights and the Wallace Candidacy of 1964

When the civil rights movement began in the mid-1950s with the Montgomery, Alabama, bus boycott and lunch-counter sit-ins, most Wisconsin residents, black as well as white, viewed it as a Southern problem that "can't happen here." Nevertheless, the rights movement spread north in the 1960s, and the issues changed. In the South the fight had involved racial segregation enforced by law; in the North it was a matter of segregation imposed by custom and prejudice.

Milwaukee was one of the most racially segregated cities in the country. Large numbers of blacks had moved into the city after World War II, and by the 1960s they numbered 15 percent of the population. Although racial covenants were not legally enforceable, neighborhood hostility and blacks' own poverty drove them into the central-city ghetto. Most held unskilled or semiskilled jobs in "service" and "private household" occupations—census bureau euphemisms for cooks, dishwashers, hospital orderlies, waiters and bartenders. Even those in the construction industry were "general" workers and not carpenters, bricklayers or masons. In Madison, a city of mobile professionals, they fared somewhat better. In 1963 the *Wisconsin State Journal* reported that Madison's black community had two attorneys, four teachers, six or eight ministers, one professor and several instructors at the university.

Residential segregation in Milwaukee inevitably resulted in segregated schools. In 1960 a survey by the NAACP found that, in the central city, one high school, two junior high schools and 11 elementary schools were more than 90 percent black. The black schools were staffed principally by black teachers, due to a school board policy of assigning teachers to schools near their homes. Wisconsin's white population nevertheless watched the commotion in other states with complacency until August 28, 1963, when the Congress of Racial Equality (CORE), a younger and more militant organization than the NAACP, organized a civil rights demonstration in Milwaukee. It was the first such action in Wisconsin's modern history. CORE timed the assemblage to coincide with a larger demonstration at the Lincoln Memorial in Washington, D.C., which was addressed by Martin Luther King. In May 1964 the protesters organized a boycott of the black ghetto schools, and more than half of the black students joined in. The *Milwaukee Journal* described it as "well organized and well controlled [without] a single disorderly incident." Nevertheless, the protests, and the rhetoric that inevitably accompanied them, left many whites in Milwaukee and elsewhere in Wisconsin uncomfortable. They showed their distress in the primary elections that spring.

Father James Groppi leading a school desegregation demonstration, Milwaukee, 1967.

1964 was a presidential election year. Lyndon Johnson, having succeeded the assassinated John F. Kennedy, was seeking voter approval for a term of his own. George Wallace entered the contest for the Democratic nomination, capitalizing on a white "backlash" against the growing militancy of the civil rights movement. Wallace had come to national attention as governor of Alabama by standing in "the schoolhouse door" in order to prevent blacks from entering the University of Alabama. Although his was essentially an appeal to prejudice, he cloaked his racial stance with a sensible-sounding conservatism. The only difference in the South's legal segregation and the North's de facto segregation, he told a group of

Protestant ministers in Oshkosh, was that "in the South, we believe in segregation and say so." He did not mention black people; instead he campaigned against civil rights legislation then under consideration by Congress, contending that it would result in undue federal interference in local government. A powerful speaker with a facility for telling audiences what they wanted to hear, Wallace was greeted by enthusiastic crowds, culminating in a triumphant meeting at Serb Hall on Milwaukee's South Side on April 1. "If I ever have to leave Alabama," he told his audience, "I'd want to live on the South Side of Milwaukee."

In the election Wallace astonished the nation by winning 34 percent of the vote in the Democratic primary. The backbone of his strength, to be sure, was among blue-collar workers who feared for their jobs, neighborhoods and schools. But, as in 1960, there was a large Republican crossover. Wealthy, suburban Waukesha County led all the counties in the state in the proportion of its vote that went to Wallace. It is thus evident that Wallace's appeal went beyond the narrow bounds of racial prejudice. He was perceived as a man who believed in limited federal government and strong local authority. He gave expression to the mounting frustration with the growing burden of taxes and the expanding social welfare state. As a result, he touched a chord that was still reverberating in Wisconsin 30 years later.

Civil rights leaders were experiencing frustrations of their own by the mid-1960s. Federal laws enacted in 1964 and 1965 protected black voting rights and opened job opportunities for blacks and women, but the inertia of a large and generally well-to-do populace held progress to a glacial pace. Black frustration generated urban violence. Beginning with the Los Angeles enclave of Watts in 1965, inner-city riots became an annual affair. On the night of July 30, 1967, a week after arson and violence laid waste to a large part of the city of Detroit, Milwaukee's inner core erupted. When police moved in to quell a small disturbance, their cars were stoned, and the rock-throwing soon extended to white-owned stores. When it became apparent that the police could not control the situation, the governor called out the National Guard. The violence lasted for eight days, and by the time it was over four people had been killed and more than 1,500 arrested. Milwaukee's riot ranked behind only those in Detroit and Newark among "civil disorders" in that most violent of years.

Following the riot were daily demonstrations through the winter of 1967-68 for open housing and school integration ordinances. Leader of the marches was a white Catholic priest, Father James E. Groppi. Although Groppi himself was an abrasive, uncompromising personality who aroused a great deal of white hostility, the 200 days of consecutive marches did dramatize the seriousness of the racial gap that divided Milwaukee. On March 30, 1968, the Milwaukee Common Council relented and passed a strong open-housing ordinance, prohibiting discrimination in nearly all rental housing. Adoption of the ordinance ended the militant civil rights movement in Milwaukee, but it proved by no means a panacea. Twenty-five years later Milwaukee was still a segregated city with a record of poverty, unemployment and violence at its inner core.

▼

Vietnam and the 1968 Democratic Primary

Civil rights activism merged in the mid-1960s into an anti-war movement as President Johnson escalated the American presence in Vietnam. The war protests originated on university campuses, and the Madison campus was in the forefront. Many of the students who led the movement had been "radicalized" by their experience in helping Southern blacks to desegregate public facilities and register to vote earlier in the decade. By the summer of 1967, when Johnson sent an additional 45,000 men to Vietnam and asked for higher taxes to finance the war, Democratic liberals—who had solidly backed the Truman-Eisenhower-Kennedy policy of containing communism—were having serious misgivings. Highly respected Sen. William Fulbright called the war "unnecessary and immoral," and he blamed it for sidetracking the nation from its grave domestic problems. Professors at Madison and other state institutions conducted "teach-ins," public forums outside of class in which they sought to explain the background and mistaken assumptions of America's intervention in Southeast Asia.

1968 would be a presidential election year, and during the winter Minnesota's Sen. Eugene McCarthy announced his anti-war candidacy for the Democratic nomination. New Hampshire's early-March primary was the nation's first. Neither McCarthy nor Johnson was on the ballot (the president had yet to declare himself officially a candidate), so voters had to write down their choice. With an army of young people passing out literature and canvassing door to door, McCarthy, unknown in the state a few weeks before, won 42 percent of the vote (to the president's 49 percent). This astounding outcome in a very conservative state induced Sen. Robert Kennedy to enter the Democratic race as another anti-war candidate.

The next stop for all candidates was Wisconsin, whose primary was scheduled for April 2. McCarthy arrived in the state with more money, students and prestige than he had in New Hampshire. Madison was in an uproar, with weekly demonstrations by anti-war activists, their ranks swelled by nonpolitical youngsters who simply did not want to be drafted and sent off to a hopeless war. The president, whose candidacy was yet to be announced, sent an advance man into Madison to test the political climate. He apparently got lost in the turmoil. "All we've heard from him," confessed a Johnson campaign strategist, "is a faint bleep, like the last signal from the Bay of Pigs." On March 31 President Johnson, rather than face Wisconsin's voters, startled the world by announcing that he would not seek re-election as president. He halted the bombing of North Vietnam and opened peace negotiations.

▼

Looking Ahead

Wisconsin's political history in the ensuing decades was, by contrast, remarkably placid. The state's social problems have endured, but neither political party has made a serious effort to address them. The reason, perhaps, is that the problems of modern society defy easy solution. And the cure often presents new and unexpected challenges. A few examples will suffice.

Electric power. Whether or not Wisconsin's population increases, electricity is the "steam power" of the modern "industrial revolution" and the key to the state's future development. (This book is being written on a word processor on a farm that did not even have electric power 50 years ago.) Yet "cheap" power comes at considerable cost. Production of electricity by damming rivers causes thermal pollution, by the use of coal causes air pollution, and by the use of nuclear energy causes problems of waste disposal. There is no completely satisfactory option.

Following the Badgers' Rose Bowl victory, Mike Leckrone leads the UW Marching Band in its famed Fifth Quarter performance.

Native Americans. Wisconsin's Indian population, once the poorest and most degraded element in the state, has thrived in the last 20 years on the proceeds from casino gambling—legally permitted by a crease in the tricornered sovereignty of tribal, state and federal governments. The tribes, for the most part, seem to have invested the money wisely—in durable industries, shopping centers and schools for their children. But the social cost is high, for gambling is a "tax" paid (albeit willingly) often by those who can least afford it, and it can lead to compulsive behavior that has to be treated at the expense of society.

Dairy farming. Since World War II the number of dairy farms in Wisconsin has declined steadily, and the family farm as an

American institution seems to be in danger of extinction. The movement from farm to city has been going on for 200 years, yet it has now reached the point where the rural lifestyle, and all its aesthetic values, seems to be threatened. What to do? The dairy industry has declined in part because its products—meat, milk and eggs—contain high levels of fats and cholesterol that are dangerous to health. What is the social price of maintaining the family farm? What to do? The political system, to date, has no answers.

Perhaps the measure of the tranquillity of Wisconsin's society and politics in the 1980s and early 1990s is the excitement generated by the turnaround in the university's sports program. It is quite possible, after all, that the event of the decade was the 1993 Big-Ten co-championship and the Rose Bowl victory on January 1, 1994.

On Wisconsin!

▼

Travelers' Guide

Babcock Hall, University of Wisconsin, 1605 Linden Dr., Madison; (608) 262-3045. Enjoy one of the UW Food Science Department's most famous products—ice cream, made right on campus. Buy a cone or sundae at the dairy bar, then watch the processing operation from a second-floor balcony. Nearby is the Old Campus Dairy Barn, built in 1897, and the site of pioneering research on vitamins.

Franklin Lake Campground, Nicolet National Forest, east of Eagle River on Highway 70, south on FR 2178 to FR 2181; (715) 362-1300. On the National Register of Historic Places, the campground contains log and stone buildings constructed by the Civilian Conservation Corps in 1936.

For a guide to hiking, skiing and nature trails in the Nicolet, or for a brochure on auto tours, contact the Forest Supervisor's Office, Nicolet National Forest, 68 S. Stevens St., Rhinelander, WI 54501; (715) 362-1300.

SUGGESTED READING

Two good introductions to the impact of the glacier on Wisconsin are Gwen Schultz, *Ice Age Lost* (1974), and Lee Clayton and John Attig, *Glacial Lake Wisconsin* (1989). Lawrence Martin, *The Physical Geography of Wisconsin* (1965) is scholarly and ponderous, but it contains a wealth of information.

George I. Quimby pioneered the study of Native American cultures, and his *Indian Life in the Upper Great Lakes* (1960) is a classic. *The Chippewas of Lake Superior* (1979) by Edmund Jefferson Danziger Jr. is a good study of one tribe. New discoveries and new interpretations are rapidly changing the field of Native American studies. Among the most recent studies are Robert E. Ritzenthaler and Lynne G. Goldstein, *Prehistoric Indians of Wisconsin* (1985) and Helen Hornbeck Tanner, ed., *Atlas of Great Lakes Indian History* (1987). Carol Devens has taken a novel and interesting approach in *Countering Colonization: Native American Women and Great Lakes Missions, 1630-1900* (1992).

The standard work on the exploration and early development of Wisconsin is Alice E. Smith, *History of Wisconsin: From Exploration to Statehood* (1973), volume I of an excellent six-volume history of the state. Also worthwhile is John A. Caruso, *The Mississippi Valley Frontier: The Age of Exploration and Settlement* (1966). Alice E. Smith's biography of *James Duane Doty, Frontier Promoter* (1954) provides colorful details of the Wisconsin Territory's political wars. The stories of people who moved to Wisconsin prior to the Civil War can be found in Stewart H. Holbrook, *The Yankee Exodus: An Account of Migration from New England* (1950), and Theodore C. Blegan, *Norwegian Migration to America, 1825-1860* (1940).

The standard account of the middle decades of the 19th century is Richard N. Current, *The History of Wisconsin, Volume II: The Civil War Era, 1848-1873* (1976). Wisconsin's prewar fight with the federal government is recounted in James I. Clark, *Wisconsin Defies the Fugitive Slave Law: The Case of Sherman Booth* (1955). The state's contribution to the Northern war effort is told by Frank L. Klement, *Wisconsin and the Civil War* (1963), and Alan T. Nolan, *The Iron Brigade* (1961). See also Sam Ross, *The Empty Sleeve: A Biography of Lucius Fairchild* (1964).

A nice, readable account of the logging years is Robert F. Fries, *Empire in Pine: The Story of Lumbering in Wisconsin, 1830-1900* (1951). The Rev. Peter Pernin's eyewitness account of the great Peshtigo fire is to be found in the *Wisconsin Magazine of History*, volume 54. Eric Lampard's *Rise of the Dairy Industry in Wisconsin* (1962) is heavy reading but remains the standard work.

Robert La Follette's 1911 *Autobiography* is the source of the idea that La Follette revolutionized the politics of Wisconsin. David P. Thelen provides a more critical estimate of the man and his legacy in *Robert M. La Follette and the Insurgent Spirit* (1976). The best account of Wisconsin in the 1920s and '30s is Paul Glad, *The History of Wisconsin, Volume V: The Great War, The New Era, and the Great Depression, 1914-1940* (1990). Also rewarding is John E. Miller, *Governor Phillip F. La Follette, the Wisconsin Progressives, and the New Deal* (1982).

For recent events in the Badger State see William F. Thompson, *The History of Wisconsin, Volume VI: Continuity and Change, 1940-1965* (1988). Thomas C. Reeves, *Life and Times of Joe McCarthy* (1982) supercedes all previous studies of the man. There are no general studies of the civil rights and anti-war movements in Wisconsin in the 1960s, but a worthwhile recent monograph is Tom Bates, *Rads: The 1970 Bombing of the Army Math Research Center at the University of Wisconsin and Its Aftermath* (1992).

INDEX

MORE BOOKS ON WISCONSIN
FROM WISCONSIN TRAILS

BARNS OF WISCONSIN
by Jerry Apps and Allen Strang

MILLS OF WISCONSIN
by Jerry Apps and Allen Strang

BEST WISCONSIN BIKE TRIPS
by Phil Van Valkenberg

BEST CANOE TRAILS OF
SOUTHERN WISCONSIN
by Michael E. Duncanson

GREAT GOLF IN WISCONSIN
by John Hughes and Jeff Mayers

Wisconsin Trails
P.O. Box 5650
Madison, WI 53705
(800) 236-8088